She is Magic, Always

A Magical Collaboration of 27 Women Sharing their Magic with the World

She is Magic Book Series
Blair Hayse Publishing
a Division of Blair Hayse,
International, LLC

This book is dedicated to all those who have magic inside them and use it to profoundly impact the world around them. I truly believe that every person has magic in them, whether they have realized it or not. I encourage you to dig deep and find that magic. Use it to spread hope to the world around you and sprinkle it wherever you may go.

So, do not be fooled, I promise,

there is magic within each of you.

Enjoy the magic in the pages within...

Table of Contents

Introduction

Blair Hayse

WHEN I HAD THE VISION OF BEGINNING THE *SHE IS Magic* book series, I had no idea we would get this far. Here we are preparing our third book to launch just this year. Each book has been filled with magical authors who I would not have met if it was not for this project. Women who are looking to make an impact in the world in a massive way. Women who shine so brightly that they cannot help but share it with the world around them. Each book I am moved to tears, laughter and tons of good memories as we move through the process of a dream to finished product. The surreal moment when they achieve best-selling author is always my favorite moment by far. Seeing them in that raw monumental moment makes everything I do worth it. It reminds me time and time again why I love my job so immensely.

This book was no different. Women from all over the world met in a moment of destiny to share magic in the world on a profound level. They joined together to make an impact greater than one could envision. They chose to unite on this journey and become vulnerable to share their stories with each of you. As I read through the stories of this book, I found myself in tears just like the books prior to this one. These women not only was raw and authentic, but they allowed that to be shared in a written form with people all of over the world. They surrendered from the ego and allowed their story of magic to shine through with each of you reading this book. Hoping that their story will touch a life and bring inspiration to those who read it.

Writing has always been something I loved to do. I could spend hours writing and time would seem to pass by quickly. I have known since I was a child that writing was my passion and even then held the dream of becoming an author one day. I had no idea that my passion would bring together 60 women in just this year alone to reach best-selling author status with me. That I would help others find the passion of writing and achieve their dream of being published. I am thankful every single day that I get to do this for a living. That I get to write, publish and share on such a massive scale. I am thankful for choosing to align with my purpose in a way that I have been able to help so many others share their story with the world. Some days I want to pinch myself to see if this is real.

Thank you to you, the reader. Without your support these ladies would not be best-selling authors. They would not be able to fulfill their dreams. We would not be able to continue to launch successfully time and time again. Thank you for following us, reading our books, writing the reviews, and sharing this with others. You are the reason we continue to do what we do. We hope to continue to bring you stories of magic and inspiration. We hope you will find your own magic as you read the books and we welcome you to join us in sharing one day if you wish to do so.

Thank you to you, the authors. Without all of you magical ladies trusting me to take you on this journey we would not have the book series. Thank you for being willing to be vulnerable and share your story with the world. I know that is not easy and can be really frightening. You have not let that fear stop you. You felt it and dove right into it because you knew you had to share your story. May each of you never forget that *"You are Magic."*

Thank you to my children Parker, Millie, and Jackson who inspire me each day to keep pursuing my dream so I can leave you a legacy behind. Thank you to my parents David and Teresa, who have always encouraged me to write and pursue my love for the literary arts. Thank you to my nanny Amanda, who watches my son each day so I can write and know he is well taken care of while I do so. Thank you to all my coaches, mentors, and teachers, all of you have impacted my life in massive ways as you helped me to become the person I am and continue to help me grow into the person I need to be. Thank you to the divine inspiration given to me from above so that I can continue to help others. Thank you to my editing team, Jennifer and Amanda, without you I would not be able to put these books out in the quality they are. Thank you to all of my staff behind the scenes who make this all happen with each role they step into. Thank you to Lane, who designs the beautiful book cover each time that represents the message inside it. Thank you to Janet, who formats each book and loads it into the system so that we have a successful launch. There are so many magical souls who have helped mold this book in the most amazing way. Thank you to my mentor Gabby Bernstein, who taught me the inspiration of my chapter, Lenses of Love in this particular book. You taught me to see things through the eyes of love and for that I have been able to heal in a way I never thought possible.

Most of all, thank you to my amazing husband Jeremy. Without your continued support this dream would not be possible. You have pulled the slack so that I can pursue this passion and have encouraged me when others left me behind. You always believed in me. You always have been my biggest fan and I want you to know I love you deeply. I am grateful for you each day that goes by. All that you say and do, never goes unnoticed. You keep me centered when I so easily can get off course.

If you are looking for something to read that is going to make you cry and laugh at the same time because it is so raw…then this book is for you. You will literally feel the emotions intertwined through these stories as you read them. These women held nothing back as they shared with you some of their innermost struggles, points of healing, lowest moments and highest accomplishments. They are authentic throughout their stories. They take you on the journey with them and you will not want to put it down as you begin to read.

As you read, be aware of your own stories found inside of you. Be aware of how sharing that story can inspire others and give others hope. It is more than just a "story." It is a journey of victory. It is a story of magic that you can sprinkle wherever you choose to go. Leave others with hope and inspiration just by being you. Never…I repeat…NEVER…hide your magic. You are Magic.

In summary this book…

It is filled with hope.

It is filled with inspiration.

It is filled with love.

It is filled with healing.

It is filled with stories of women who rise up.

It is filled with lots of magic.

Enjoy and know that this book is filled with lots of love just for you.

SHE IS MAGIC: A MAGICAL COLLABORATION OF 27 WOMEN
SHARING THEIR MAGIC WITH THE WORLD

The Power of the Human Spirit

Toni Gonzalez

HEADQUARTERS...I AM GETTING FLAGGED DOWN. Looks like a fight or something. The radio clicks. The silence I knew, and I was familiar with it. I felt like something wasn't right. Silence on a police radio means that the cop is in trouble. When you hear a call for a fight, everyone goes. This is about Officer safety. You want to make sure they are not alone in this.

I was already in my police car getting ready for my shift. I put the car in drive and pressed the gas pedal as hard as I could. I was driving there with lights and sirens, my heart was pounding, and I was looking straight ahead. I am gripping the steering wheel hard that my knuckles are white. I hear a female voice say gun. The radio went silent again. Other officers are asking questions on the police radio, but there is no answer. No one can make contact with the officers, and the silence is killing me inside. I felt like I couldn't get there fast enough.

My mind was racing.

I silently say to myself, "They are dead. They are dead. They are dead."

I finally get there which seemed like an eternity and I see a car blocking the road, and I go to grab my M-4. I ran inside the restaurant with the rifle. My eyes searched for the officers. I couldn't see them, but I saw the man. He was dead. His head leaned back where he sat eating. Blood was everywhere, and there were still many people inside the restaurant. A woman was screaming loudly, and I could tell she was in shock. A young girl was walking around in the blood. I looked down and the two offices were on the ground. I slowly looked towards their heads up from their feet, following their pant line, afraid of what I was going to see.

They were alive. They were alive.

They were holding down the suspect who had tried to disarm one of the officers. I had to stop. The smell of the blood was affecting me. I had been doing this job for over twenty years, and I didn't understand what was happening to me. I walked out. I just needed to regroup.

This was a tough day for me. You see the guy that was killed, he told me that this was how he was going to be killed. The guy came into our headquarters a few times to tell police officers that he believed this guy was going to kill him. He told me that he believed the guy bought an illegal gun and that he was going to kill him. This man, who was killed, was a protector. He wanted to protect this lady and her child from an evil man. Needless to say, he was killed for it.

The killer's daughter saw the whole thing.

When I arrived, she was walking around with a look in her eye that I was familiar with. She was walking around in the blood, looking at the guy whose brains were blown away.

She saw her father kill a man in cold blood in a crowded restaurant in broad daylight. That little girl was me.

You see when I was a little girl, someone shot my dad as he held me. I remember hearing screams, the loud bang just like it happened yesterday. The smell of the blood took my breath away. Just like when I was a little girl covered in my dad's blood, I had to walk out.

The days that followed were truly hard for me. I couldn't sleep and I was having a hard time processing the scene. Not one person asked me if I needed to talk to someone. In the middle of all of that, I was really sick and was battling a bad upper respiratory infection that was kicking my ass. As I am processing this, I get called into the office. I was being criticized for my tactics and they said I put everyone in danger.

I said what?

You gotta be kidding me.

It's been exactly one week since the incident, and I was getting called a train wreck.

Whatever happened to caring about a person after being in an incident like this?

Why was no one asking what was going on?

Do you need to talk to anyone?

You've never done anything like this, what's going on?

No nothing.

It was you are this and that and that's that.

I remember picking up a book by Don Juan Miguel Ruiz Jr., Living a life of awareness: Daily Meditations on the Toltec path. The book contained a collection of meditations and prayers. I have always been a reader and in my most trying moments I have reached for books to help me relax, or figure things out. As a matter of fact, that's what led me into this path of wellness and started my journey on helping first responders learn how to deal with stress.

I decided one day to go live in my Facebook group. I had started a group called *"Wellness for You"*, to help First Responders deal with stress. This wasn't easy in this world you are judged quite often not only by the public, but by the people you work with. You get labeled and that label stays with you. It's the equivalent of being bullied in high school. I hit live and that day, and I spoke about not letting anyone dull your sparkle. This Facebook Live was about pushing past the B.S. that people put in front of you. The importance of knowing how valuable you are even in the darkest hour.

That video has over 890 views.

I thought to myself people need to hear this.

I set out to make sure that I shared a daily message with everyone.

This was a real thing for me.

This incident left me feeling attacked, but I didn't want to go down the road that was truly familiar for me. One filled with anger, numbing out, and trying to suppress my feelings. I didn't want to do that. I worked really hard after being sick and having brain surgery. I didn't want to waste my life staying angry, not forgiving people and using my energy unwisely. It was an eye-opening experience to have been sick, recovered, and given a second chance at life. A second chance to get it right and help others.

The things that happened to me and all of the trials
that I went through, taught me that I had a bigger purpose.
I was here to change the way that first responders are
treated. There aren't many services out here to help them
and that when they do seek help, they are ostracized: that
should never happen.

"Wellness for You" morphed into *"Mindfulness for
First Responders"* and created a resiliency room for my
department. The resiliency room is a place for a first
responder to sit in and have peace and quiet when
needed. They can perhaps listen to music to relax during
their break, or maybe request that someone speak to
them in a private setting. Not all bad things, stay bad. I
created a podcast where I shared book readings, tips on
dealing with stress, breathing techniques, meditation
and interviews of officers who have retired from law
enforcement or are currently working. I talk about the
power of using music, laughter, blowing bubbles, adult
coloring and other things that are super easy to carry
with you , which enables you to do them anywhere.
I talk about using essential oils can shift your mood,
even in your police car, and how coloring or doodling
in your car before qualification can help you relax.
That's what I decided to do with my experience: to help
first responders relieve their stress with the things I had
tried myself.

What I learned from this experience made me realize that we do not focus enough on the mental health of First Responders.

Think about this.

They see more than anyone will ever see in their entire lifetime.

This is something they do every day of their careers. Some officers stay thirty years or more. Some states don't have a limit and retirement can be at the age of sixty-five. That means that you can do over forty years of this work.

This is not good.

Who checks on the officers after their calls?

No one.

I became numb, angry, and at times would just zone out other times after all these incidents.

It is important to have systems in place that help officers decompress and have a moment of privacy. Why is that important? There are times that a call can take you from being totally calm to feeling like you can't control yourself. You can be sitting in a car having a peaceful conversation, and within seconds everything changes. It can go from peace to pure chaos. This happens for an entire career. The fact is officers need to decompress. It's important. Officers do not become violent overnight, angry overnight, or numb overnight. People don't stop to think that what First Responders have experienced could be attributed to those self-destructive behaviors. Seeing a dead baby who has just been murdered by a parent for no good reason is not something you will ever forget. That feeling of "I can't cry right now," but you are thinking of your child at home. I thought of my son many times as I handled those calls that tore at my soul. I thought, how could someone do this? These are things that as humans we relate to our own experiences.

How you make sure that officers are doing well is by checking in on them. This is important because most of the time we focus on people after they have become a problem. You may have an officer that is drinking a lot or getting many complaints against them. The department "deals" with them, but are they "dealing" with the real problem? There aren't enough ways to check on officers without someone feeling like they are infringing on their rights. Checking in is a way to make sure that they don't hurt anyone or themselves.

My journey to wellness was not an easy route for me. I found myself in places that I could not believe I was in. I hid my emotions with anger, and I isolated myself from the world. The pain I felt was too much to talk about and I pushed people away. After reading many books, this was a sign that my brain wasn't processing all the information that way that it should have.

Therapy was my go-to place. I was fortunate enough to have met a therapist that understood cops and she was not letting me get away with nonsense. She understood me, she understood the job, and she understood the politics in the job. I had an opportunity to get my life in order and to see my worth. You often lose sight of yourself when you are dealing with everyone else's problems, their pain, and their lives.

The resiliency room is where officers can go to relax. This is a piece of the puzzle that most people don't find. What I am trying to explain is that people treat First Responders as if they are machines and they shouldn't feel things, be upset, or act human. Instead, they are expected to just perform, do what they need, and then move on. That isn't the case. They are human beings, with real human lives, real human problems and sometimes we bring those to work. It is part of living.

I can tell you from my own experience that I went through many things at work, but also in my personal life. I went through a tough divorce and I worked with him as well. Now let's talk about him marrying one of my co-workers and then I was her boss. Isn't that stressful? Right?! It was stressful. It tore at me every time I dealt with it. It was not only stressful but a kick in the gut. I had to work under those conditions, and there were times, I felt I wasn't getting a break anywhere I went. The piece of having a release, a respite is necessary. There are people who don't have that at home. Having a place to sit and relax for a few minutes is key.

There are other pieces of relaxation that must be incorporated in this profession and that starts with teaching officers of the damage that this type of work does to the human spirit. From personal example: At one point in my career, I was angry, and I hid my feelings with anger. I was abrasive and when someone cried in front of me, I didn't feel anything. This part of the job should not be normal or referred to as part of the job.

This is a recipe for disaster. You start unraveling in ways that you are not prepared for. You feel things that you've never felt before. Mental health is not something that just some people go through. This is a huge part of a First Responder's life. This is why I am a big believer in mental health, therapy, relaxation, resiliency rooms, and talking it out.

I can tell you that the person I am today, is not the person I was years ago. Some would say, "Duh, none of us are the same person." To those that say that, I want to tell them this: I walked into a profession that didn't explain much about what I was going to feel. Read that again.

I was told how to run, how to work out, how to study, how to memorize laws, and how to take tests, but no one prepared me for what I would feel. Now, my family was similar to this. No one ever talked about how they felt. Crying was a sign of weakness, and we basically tiptoed around serious issues.

Expressing our feelings is an important part of processing our emotions. This was the HARDEST part for me to learn and to process. Therapy helped me see this clearly. Life lessons helped me feel. If we go into a job thinking this isn't part of it, we are in for a rude awakening. We must be okay with telling a person that they can feel. That you can cry if you want to. That you can scream if you want to. That you can be sad if you want to. That you are not getting over it by ignoring it. That if you suppress it and you are creating a bomb.

My bomb exploded when I got divorced. I had so many emotions inside that I didn't want to function anymore. After three days in bed, my brother came over and said, "You need to get up." "You can't quit." You can't let them win. It was so hard to get up. I felt like a failure, I was embarrassed at work, and I felt alone and defeated. I recognized it and called my therapist. I said, "I can't do this." I need help and I need someone to guide me. Thankfully that is exactly what she did. I had fallen hard. It wasn't only the divorce, it was the job, it was family, it was everything that had anything to do with life. Without her help and techniques, I would not be the person I am today. Therapy not only helped me, but allowed me to be able to help others in my profession who need the support.

We must be given an opportunity to feel. We are human. We are like everyone else out here except we wear invisible capes.

ABOUT TONI GONZALEZ

It all starts with you. Toni Gonzalez has been a police officer for over 24 years. She has a bachelor's degree in Health and Wellness and a Masters in the Science of Criminal Justice. She is passionate about Wellness for First Responders and teaching First Responders how to use mindfulness tools to relieve their stress. She created a Resiliency room for her Police department and was nominated to receive the Detective Pablo Santiago Resiliency Award from the Attorney General in New Jersey. She continues to share tips on Facebook on the *Wellness for You* page and at *Mindfulness for First Responders*. She blogs occasionally and hosts a podcast Wellness for You and Alexa Flash Briefing with tips. Her website hosts many different tips, suggestions, and courses:

www.itsmetoni.com.

She reminds officers to do something daily to relieve their stress and not to wait for a day off.

Today is the perfect day to start.

Dear You,

Ally Bishop

Dear You,

How did we get here?

I have always longed for your love... for your approval.

Where did we go wrong?

My heart aches to know you better. I feel like I never truly have. You never let me in.

So many questions burn inside my body everyday about you.

How come your vibe doesn't match your actions?

When did lying become so easy for you?

I feel so close to you, yet I barely know you.

How can I say I have someone so close to me that I truly don't know?

You have never allowed me in. You have never reached out to become better and anytime you did you'd tell me everything you thought I wanted to hear.

How you want to be better.

How you want to fix your mistakes, but you still continue to prove otherwise with your actions. It must feel so lonely. It must feel so confusing and messy.

Tearing me down made you feel better, didn't it?

Where did you learn such behavior?

Where did you learn it was okay to treat women like that?

Through you, I learned I lost myself, but also how much empathy I possess.

Behind closed doors, that's the energy you have deep within. But to everyone else, you're emotionally unavailable. You don't let anyone in.

You used to act like everything was fine, but behind my back told everyone how much I didn't mean to you. Why?

I've always feared I'd never truly get to know you.

My heart aches with pain knowing I'll never understand who you truly are. Emotionally unavailable, and I feel I am no longer available to try.

Dear You,

It's in my blood to always care. Even when at times I have to pretend I don't care. I still care. No matter how many times you hurt me. No matter how many times you don't truly care... I just can't not love you.

It is so hard to want to open up the walls that keep you so hidden. I feel like I will never truly know you. I will never be allowed in. I don't know if anyone will ever be allowed in. It must feel so lonely where you keep yourself. Just thinking of you living in that vast loneliness pains me more than any of the pain you caused me. The fiery anger you hold within you. That anger that causes everyone around you to walk on eggshells. That anger that makes everyone afraid of what you might do or say. Afraid they might never see you again. Afraid you might never come back.

How can someone feel so attached to another, yet so unattached at the same time? I guess that's how the wrong relationships work, huh?

Out of my own bad habits, holding on to you so tightly felt better than letting go. Letting go always felt mean, rude, and cruel.

Where did this pain come from?

I almost want to punch anyone who has ever done this to you. I want to protect you from any pain that you have ever received or any darkness that has latched onto you. I just question where it came from? What life? It couldn't possibly be this one, could it? Then again, I would never know. I don't truly know you. I want to know you, but I don't think I ever will.

The glimpses of hope shine through you and make me believe that you are there. Those small moments of hope cause me to get attached to that unrequited love again. It's a vicious cycle like a drug. You are exactly like a drug. Once you have had a taste of the love you can give, you always search for that high again. Then as if by clockwork, then the manipulation comes out. The manipulation comes out and it affects me. It drains me. It confuses me, but it leaves me wanting more. Leaves me hoping that one day you'll help me understand you. Leaves me wanting to feel loved by you because I think I've felt it before, but I don't know if it was actually love or just what I always thought love was.

You know, drugs don't just affect one person. They affect all the people around them. They affect every single person in their circle on a daily basis. I always thought I was just overreacting, but anytime those boundaries were set you would get angry. Really angry. You made me feel awful for not prioritizing your needs. I figured love meant sacrificing your needs to make others happy. The only time I ever felt true authentic love from you is when I would hug you. I could feel you asking me to help you internally, but anytime I brought it up you would shrug me away or not open up. Anytime we would talk on a deeper level, you would tell me how much you want to change. I felt those glimpses of hope shining once again. Until weeks later, it would be the same story all over again.

I was always looking for the approval of male figures in my life, like I needed to be a certain someone in order to get their attention. Something about letting new male figures into my life never felt safe. It always felt like a chase or I would have to mask my true self in order to gain their approval first. I dodged most situations like that, avoiding any situation I was put in that didn't feel safe or secure. I felt as if there was some type of agenda because I had male figures in my life who were extremely emotionally unavailable, I constantly attracted that into my life.

Anytime I let my guard down to a new male figure, I felt there was an agenda or a chance to be taken advantage of. It wasn't long until I met someone else who did all of those things. Took advantage of me, used me, manipulated me, loved me, and was also emotionally unavailable. I don't know why I let it go on for so long, maybe because I felt if I could break open and understand this particular soul, I could finally understand you. It was like some sort of challenge.

After three intense years of soul searching, I finally understood the meaning of my power. It took years to understand because I used to cry at everything. I cried when I was happy, when I was sad, when I was angry. Tears would just effortlessly flow out of me. It is almost like I could not put an end to them. I remember when I was younger being called a cry baby, so I learned right then and there how to suppress my emotions in order to survive. I spent most of my teenage years trying to fix you, but feeling I wasn't doing a good job. So, I would try and fix everyone else, as a way to make up for what I couldn't do for you. Like a leaky faucet, I didn't know how to shut the tears off. I could cry at the drop of a hat.

I didn't understand how I could produce so many tears. In order to survive high school, I had to suppress the emotions that so effortlessly came out of me to be strong for you, but to also show everyone else around me I was strong for them. I didn't want to look "too sensitive." I started to believe something was wrong with me. I finally told my Mom I thought I could be depressed, and there was the time I asked my Dad if he ever pictured swerving into a tree on purpose, too. As a teenager, I felt insecure and weak to admit it, but I truly couldn't understand where these emotions came from.

I went to countless doctors who wanted to prescribe me antidepressants. I remember my Mom's friend telling me that, "Sometimes people just don't produce as much serotonin as others, and that is okay. You should never feel ashamed for wanting to help yourself." But deep down, I felt it was more than just a pill to take. I didn't want to numb my emotions, even though a lot of people told me otherwise. I wanted to fix the root cause: the deep-rooted pain, sadness, abandonment, and anger. I persisted to figure out what the pain was, without the medication.

I researched tons on my own about anxiety, depression, ways to cope and make it go away. My Mom suggested holistic alternatives which got me curious. I started to read up on ways to get better so that I could help others, so that I could also help you.

After years of my own work, I started to understand what being an empath was. I heard it from many people, but when I really started to understand it on a deeper level, I started to understand myself. I had suppressed emotions for years, and as a teenager I didn't understand what energetic boundaries were. I was always a huge people pleaser. I understand now, I would take on other people's emotions unintentionally. I felt so deeply and intensely for any stranger that would share their pain, almost as if it were happening to me. I started studying a lot about the ego versus the true-self discovering questions such as, what projections do we cast onto the outside world from the perceptions within? What are the unhealed stories that play on the projection screens of our minds? How do these stories affect your everyday life?

Underneath the tough skin, there were painful memories tucked away. I had to UNlearn that saying no, without feeling guilty, doesn't mean you don't care about that person. It is okay to spend time alone without having to explain myself, and that it is NOT my job to rescue people from their drama. I also recognized that darkness attracts light, and when you constantly are giving yourself to others they can use you to their advantage. I started asking myself questions on where these behaviors stemmed from. Our suppressed emotions from our childhood will forever stay stuck within us if we are unwilling to do the inner work, and when we start to understand and heal ourselves on the deepest level, with so much love in our heart, we start to understand the Universe and the unity between us all. Healing younger memories of myself has allowed me to understand you, and although still painful, I am learning to let go of you so that I can finally be free.

ABOUT ALLY BISHOP

Ally grew up in the suburbs of the Lehigh Valley in Macungie, Pennsylvania. After graduating high school in 2013, she went to college at Philadelphia University to attain her Bachelor's degree in Professional Communications. She is a Certified Hatha Yoga Instructor, free spirit, loves nature, the ocean, Mexican food, and enjoys traveling to other countries with her significant other.

In her younger years, Ally was always the "good girl." As a teenager, she experimented with drugs and the law as a way of rebellion. Everything appeared to be perfect. But on the inside battled with obsessive thinking, uncontrollable emotions, depression, anxiety, and dark thoughts. Years of questioning life and her soul gifts, she committed to her own research in becoming the best woman she could be for herself and for others, who shared similar pain points.

Ally knew all her life that she wouldn't be a Corporate America girl, although had many jobs in Sales. Until one day, she courageously said, "screw it, I'm doing what makes me happy." She got her Hatha Yoga certification and thought, right then and there, she would be a full-time yoga teacher living on a beach somewhere, or so she thought. When her bank account started to reflect otherwise, she knew she'd have to sacrifice finding another job; and this time it was through a network marketing company. When she saw quick success in building a team and selling products, she was sold on, "be your own boss kind-of-life." She quickly grew within the company and soon realized that people would reach out to her more surrounding mindset, rather than products. It was in that moment when she realized a part of her was still missing. Not having any experience at all owning a business or even some of the entrepreneurial terminology, she hired her own business coaches and soon pivoted into owning her own spiritual coaching business, Ally Bishop LLC. In just 3 months of starting her own business, Ally is a booked-out healing coach having women all over the U.S. wanting to work with her deeply through their healing journeys.

Ally is highly intuitive and specializes in healing and reprogramming trauma, surrounding the Inner Child, so that her clients can eliminate self-sabotage and embody their most magnetic lives. With her highly in-tune abilities she is able to help her clients quickly access the inner limitations that keep them held back, transforming her clients deep rooted pain into clarity and unshakable confidence in who their authentic self is.

Ally offers a variety of free resources such as: free 30-minute breakthrough calls and oracle readings to women all over the U.S. She has built her sacred community solely on Instagram without a website, email list, or Facebook group. She is committed to her purpose in helping women all over the world reclaim their self-worth and embody their most authentic life.

You can connect with Ally on the following Platforms:

INSTAGRAM:
https://instagram.com/allybish0p

CALENDLY:
https://calendly.com/allybish1/1-1-breakthrough-call

The Journey from Helpless to Wholeness

Muria Nisbett

Death of my inner child

You need to go home; you can't stay here.

Nine words that have shaped the course of my life.

At the age of 8, my mom said that to me,

She was no longer my mother; she was someone's wife.

At the time that I needed her most and needed to be loved

She chose to walk away, because she had to honor her vows.

I turned and walked away hoping she would stop me

I thought that there was no way she would let me go so easily.

The feeling of shame and abandonment washed over me

As I realized her love was not available to me

She was supposed to be my home, my safety, my sanctuary,

But instead she was the reason I lived my life feeling shattered and empty.

THE JOURNEY FROM A BROKEN MOTHER-DAUGHTER relationship to a healed and loving union is not only possible, but the most beautiful transformation that you can ever experience. I know this because I have lived it and I now help others to experience this incredible journey. For me, this transformational healing came late in my life and in an instant, I was reborn and set on a new sacred journey that is now my life. I smile every day. I experience joy and happiness. I feel whole and fulfilled. Most of all, I know with absolute certainty that I am enough. The way that I experience life is in direct contrast to the person I used to be. I want to walk you through this journey with me, to see how a scared and confused little girl became a mother-daughter relationship expert helping mothers and daughters to repair their broken relationships.

There was a time in my life when I felt broken, unloved, and unnecessary. I cried myself to sleep every night and wanted to die every day. I could not figure out where I fit in this world and there was no one who cared enough to guide me. I walked through my life as a shadow, hidden in plain sight. I was passed over, neglected, and disregarded. Every day was a struggle and honestly, I was just tired. I always knew that I was different, and I thought that was a bad thing. I longed for peace, for love, and for someone to tell me that I was enough, but that never happened. I became a tumbleweed blowing in the wind. I was at the mercy of the elements, just being tossed around in search of a safe resting place.

Childhood for me was one of being in the way. I was the child who was to be neither seen nor heard. No one had time for me. No one cared to love me, hug me, and acknowledge me. Somehow in all that brokenness, I knew that there was a fire inside me that was longing to burn, if only someone would care to ignite it. On the rare occasions that I garnered the strength and courage to light my own fire, it was quickly extinguished with the harsh reminder that I was inconsequential. The people who were supposed to love me the most made me feel the worst. The ones who were supposed to be my guardians, protectors, my shield from the harshness of the world were the ones that made me hate being alive. At that young age in my life, I felt like I had indeed died. I was dead to the world and dead inside. My body was alive, but my heart and soul were dead.

My teen years were more of the same, I dragged my corpse along life's highways and byways, hoping for something or someone to make me feel alive again. I needed someone to see the value in me and let me know that I was worth being resuscitated. Instead, all I found was more confirmation that I was not worth anything. Well, I wasn't worth anything unless I was willing to be used as a doormat, so that's exactly what I became. I allowed everyone to walk all over me in exchange for any remnants of attention. I allowed myself to be available for others and make sure their needs were being met while neglecting the fact that my needs were never going to be included in this relationship. I didn't care. I played the game because at least someone was pretending to need me and pretending to care that I existed. I gave and gave of myself, until I literally had nothing left to give and I was officially broken.

At my lowest point, I realized that all I wanted and needed was the love and acceptance of my mother. I realized that my search for validation and acceptance was actually a search for my mother to embrace and value me. I realized that throughout my life she was never really there for me and never showered me with love. She never put me first and never made me a priority. She was there for everyone else and gave so much of herself to others, while I watched and envied them for getting a version of my mother that was never available to me. I watched as she poured so much love and compassion into others around me. I heard the words of acceptance and validation that should have been reserved for me, but were instead freely given to others. I listened as she praised others for their efforts and accomplishments while my equal and parallel efforts went unnoticed. It was so heartbreaking to know that nothing I did or who I was did not warrant appreciation and reverence. It was in those moments, that my self-esteem and any semblance of self-worth were stripped away.

It hurt to watch other parents show up for their kids and celebrate their accomplishments, both big and small. I felt like an orphan in my own home and a stranger in my own body. I developed the mindset that if my own mother cannot love me, then I must not be worthy of love. If my own mother did not value my existence, how could I expect the world to accept me? At the age of thirty-seven, I was still a little girl longing for the loving embrace of my mother. Only she could heal these wounds that I have carried around my entire life. No matter how much I cried, she was unable and unwilling to be there. At age thirty-seven, it became clear that my healing would have to be an inside job.

At age thirty-eight, my healing journey began. I tried everything I could think of to repair the brokenness inside me, because living as an empty shell was no longer an option. I tried counseling, but that did not work as I expected. Session after session became a source of re-traumatization, a trigger, a reminder of how I got here, and it offered no comfort. I think it's because my adult body was in the counseling session, but my mind and soul were that of the little girl longing for her mother. Counseling was not reaching her, if anything it was ignoring her existence and reminding her that how she feels was not important. I continued this process in the hopes that one day it would change, hoping it would change. I had heard many stories about how people in counseling were making great progress. Stories about how they were transforming their lives. Stories about how they were getting to a place of healing. For me, counseling felt like another thing that I had failed. There I was, with all the tools and resources that my counselor was providing and all the comforting words and compassion, but still nothing. I left every session feeling more lost, confused and empty. So, I quit.

My next move was to become a serial entrepreneur. I thought that if I created something that the world needed that I would be accepted, appreciated, and that my mother would have no choice but to notice how amazing I was. I bounced from business venture to business venture; I moved from state to state and address to address. I moved to six different states in five years searching for myself and that one great idea that would make me appear relevant, but nothing ever did. I wasn't searching for myself. I was in fact running from myself and the pain of being abandoned. That was until I found hypnotherapy. This was it, the magic bullet, the thing that transformed me into the dynamic person I am today. I was introduced to hypnotherapy while searching the web for ways to deal with childhood trauma. It sounded like something corky and unorthodox, but it was worth a try since nothing else had worked. At this point, I had nothing left to lose. Little did I know that in one session, my world would be altered in the most amazing way.

Hypnotherapy is not what many people believe it to be. It wasn't mind-control or submission, but a gateway to my inner child. In one session, I stood face to face with the eight-year-old me standing there waiting for my mother to take my hand and choose me. I looked into her eyes and saw her tears; I was able to feel the pain of the rejection. Standing there and looking at her; I was able to reach out, wipe away her tears and whisper to her the words that she longed to hear. *"You are not a burden; I will love you and protect you always. Your home is and will always be with me. You are enough and I choose you."* As I said those words to her, I reached out, grabbed her hands and walked her away from all the pain and sorrow. I welcomed her into my world. I let her know that she no longer has to live on that doorstep waiting for love that was never coming, but instead, she now lives with me in my world where love, happiness, joy, and acceptance will always be available to her. I embraced her so tightly that I felt her merge into my heart. She was now a part of me and never again will she have to question her worth or question where she belongs. She belongs with me. By the end of the session, we both cried, but this time it was tears of joy and completion.

For the next twenty-one days after that session, my life started to change for the better. For the first time in my life, I knew who I was and where I belonged. The pain of rejection was replaced by a feeling of acceptance that I had never experienced. I was seeing and experiencing life from a place of wholeness. Let me tell you… it was amazing.

It was from this place that I was able to approach my mother... not to seek her love, but I instead approached her with forgiveness and understanding that she was probably an unhealed soul incapable of showing me the love that she herself never experienced. Through this process, I learned that she had indeed experienced her own traumas and was also an unhealed child forced to live as an adult. The anger that I had held on to for three decades was now replaced with compassion. As we spoke, I saw in her the pain that I once felt and in that moment, I realized that my expectations of her were unrealistic. I expected her to give me something that she never had. I expected her to show me things that she herself had never seen. I was longing for her to accept me when she never felt accepted. All she had to offer was a generational curse of pain and self-loathing. One that was passed on to her.

The next year of our lives were better because I was whole and she was working towards a level of healing that she never thought was possible. She too was able to access her inner child and provide that love and comfort that she had been seeking. So, there we were, two hearts finally experiencing the love that we both deserved. We are becoming the best version of ourselves both together and individually. I am writing this to let you know that healing is possible and that love is available to each and every one of you. The mother daughter bond is one of the most crucial for both mother and daughter. When this bond is broken, it may lead to a life full of pain and negative self-esteem. I have encountered many mothers and daughters who feel that their relationship is beyond repair. I have heard the stories of narcissistic moms and ungrateful daughters, but their voices and demeanor tell a different story. What I hear is the story of a mother incapable of love and an unloved daughter who is trying to heal from a place where healing is not conducive. Regardless of the role assigned to you, mother or daughter, we are all humans searching for love and belonging. Being a loving mother can be difficult if you have never experienced love. In the same respect, a daughter who is unloved may coast through life in search of love in any shape or form that appears to be available. It is important to remember that as a mother, it is not your job to fix your daughter and form her into what you feel she should be. As a daughter, it is not your job to heal the wounds of your mother. Healing is an inside job and only from a place of healing and wholeness can you truly emerge as the best version of yourself.

My transformation is an ongoing process and each day I grow and learn and make the best of each moment. I now feel the freedom to live my life unapologetically; knowing that I am loved and my inner child is at peace. All my decisions are made with her in mind and are no longer made with desperation and the need for acceptance. I make it a point to say loving things to myself each day because I know that she is always listening. I leave positive notes around the house knowing that she will see them, and they will make her heart smile. This level of happiness and healing is available to all. It is my sincere hope that you experience the liberation of this type of transformation.

ABOUT MURIA NISBETT

When you marry passion, ambition, strength and tenacity, the end result would be Muria

Nisbett. Muria is a dynamic individual with a life-long passion of bringing love and healing to everyone she meets. This passion has fueled her decision to become a hypnotherapist, licensed social worker, Reiki master, Yoga Nidra instructor, and most importantly, a mother-daughter relationship coach. Muria Nisbett was born and raised in St. Thomas Virgin Islands. Shortly after high school, she joined the US Army where she served five years and one combat deployment.

Muria is a published author and has a five -year background as a therapist and a coach. She specializes in helping adult mothers and daughters to build a happy, health, loving, and lasting relationship using hypnotherapy and personalized coaching. This passion was born out of her desire to create a healthy relationship with her own mother and daughter, and her lifelong search for wholeness and self-fulfillment.

Muria has coached countless moms and daughters whose relationships were fractured and helped them get to a place of healing both as individuals and a mother-daughter unit. This is more than a career, but in fact, her purpose in life.

Muria has created a line of products to help mothers and daughters succeed in their relationships with each other and their relationships with themselves. The Talk Bracelet helps mothers and teen daughters build a healthy relationship from the beginning, and the mother-daughter relationship workbooks are designed to help mothers and daughters get to know each other on a deeper level. Muria has made a name for herself as mother daughter relationship coaches with a track record of success.

To connect with Muria:

https://insideoutwellnesscenter.com

info@insideoutwellnesscenter.com

Facebook:

https://www.facebook.com/insideoutwellnessbeaumont

Thriving with Anxiety: A Journey Home

Jayme Velleca

Y OU KNOW THE INTERVIEW QUESTION, "WHAT ANIMAL best describes you?" If I had to pick an animal to describe me and my life, I would choose a duck. You know how they appear calm, cool, and collected; they look like they have it all together, but underneath they're paddling like hell just to keep afloat? Reflecting back, I was really great at making sure I always looked really well put together on the outside: mentally, physically, and emotionally. I kept myself so busy that I had to plan time with friends and family well in advance. Even when my anxiety and depression were really bad, I taught myself how to be "normal" and act like everything was perfectly fine. In fact, there were many times I mentioned my anxiety to co-workers only for them to tell me that they never would have known unless I said something.

Until this one day, I'll forever remember it as if it were yesterday. I was working at what I thought was my "dream job." It was three in the morning and I called one of my friends sobbing, barely able to catch my breath. I was sweating and hyperventilating. I could feel a heaviness on my chest, my heart was racing, and I felt as if I'd soon pass out. The only part of our conversation that I remember was him telling me, *"Jayme, if you hate where you're at so much, just leave. You can get a job anywhere."* He was right, but for some reason I felt like I had to stay. You see, I had worked for this company for ten years before I finally left; I felt as if they had earned my loyalty. But, back to the real story. These episodes continued to get worse over the next few weeks. I was waking up in the middle of the night having full on panic attacks that would last for hours at a time. I experienced the worst migraine I'd ever had in my life. It woke me from a dead sleep, and nothing helped to get rid of it until I decided to go to the hospital. This is when I knew it was time for a change. Before I talk about how I decided to make a radical change, I think I should take you back in time so you can understand some of the things I had already tried before taking a huge leap of faith.

Like I mentioned before, I was always known as the girl that had it all together. It was actually the flawed perception of others, because that's what I allowed them to believe. I always felt like there was something wrong with me. Which only got worse on October 19, 2009, when I was diagnosed with epilepsy. In the state of

Pennsylvania, you lose your driver's license until you can be seizure-free for six months. I lost all of my freedom. This started a downward spiral.

Shortly after being diagnosed with epilepsy, I was admitted to the hospital by a mental health professional. I remember knowing that I'd be admitted to the hospital. I talked to my mom about it before my appointment. The only problem was that I wanted help, but I wasn't ready. I wanted the pain to go away. Like. Right. Now. I didn't want to do the work and I knew exactly what to say. I remember the nurses at the hospital saying, *"I'm not sure exactly why you're here. You seem to have it all together."* Looking back, I realize how much I wasn't ready to get the help I needed. After my hospital stay, I was heavily medicated and went to therapy. I remember the therapist I was sent to started talking about religion and I walked out of his office. So, for a long time, I never went back to therapy. I thought it was bullshit, an idea that was completely based off of this one attempt at therapy.

Instead of getting the help I needed at the time...I turned to people, places, and things. Seeking outside validation was the only thing that made me feel a little bit better: drinking and getting involved in toxic relationships, specifically. I was really good at both of those things. I still remember feeling so empty. There was this empty hole inside me, and nothing was making it manageable.

The problem was that because I was so embarrassed and ashamed to share my feelings with people, I hid them from most people! I would let things get so bad...until they were unmanageable. Luckily, throughout my darkest times I did have two friends that I could share openly with about how I was feeling. When I was really struggling, I would call these two friends and they were ALWAYS there. One of my friends showed up to visit me every single day of my stay in the hospital, despite having issues with his car; he always found a way to get there. This really gave me hope and made things seem not so bad. My other friend called off work after I got out of a toxic relationship so that she could be there for me. Having those friends is what saved me from myself. I recently just started openly talking about some of these things with family members who were more upset that I never felt comfortable telling them in the first place.

After several years and several relationships later, I decided to go back to school. I was in nursing school full-time and also working a full-time job just to make ends meet. School came fairly easy to me and it kept my mind busy. So, things were going pretty well. However, I do recall a specific day. I had won an award for something at school. I was not only tired from lack of sleep, but I had terrible social anxiety. I began to sweat and have heart palpitations just because I had to walk up and get the award. I felt like a zombie, and everything was going in slow motion. I remember specifically walking up, softly thanking them, turning around, and immediately sitting back down in my seat. I didn't make eye contact with anyone. I'm not sure what started this type of anxiety to be perfectly honest but it kept getting worse from this point forward.

I truly thought I would be happy after graduating nursing school, but I still felt like something was missing. I tried working three jobs and staying busy. I jumped from relationship to relationship. Google was my best friend. Mental health is not something people openly talk about, so I'd Google things and read endlessly. I mean, I can't be the only one to have ever Googled things like: *Is it normal to feel all alone in a crowded room?* because that shit pops up as a suggested question. I went to therapy, which really helped, but only to a certain point. I felt like there was no consistency. I'd go to therapy once a week and then forget everything; I'd live my life one week, and the following week it was like I was starting all over again. I also tried so many different medications. Some made me better, some made things way worse. Even the medications that did work usually stopped working after some time, and it was more frustrating than anything else.

Looking back, I can recall one relationship I was in where I really tried to open up by talking about my thoughts and emotions. We were sitting in his room and he was playing video games. He asked me what was wrong, so I just had a full-on meltdown. I remember his reaction being so nonchalant, like it was just another day. I could not understand how my life was so "perfect" and how I still felt incomplete. I remember not feeling depressed or anxious, but I had this voice in my head that kept repeating itself: *If you ended things now, the pain would be gone.* Simple. I'm gonna be honest, this scared the shit out of me. I was so confused as to what was going on in my brain. But that moment, those feelings, thoughts, and emotions were what triggered me to go back to therapy, which then got me to transfer to my "dream job."

I was the duck, but I was drowning. At my "dream job." I was having panic attacks at three in the morning. I had to get out, and FAST! I had worked with other nurses that traveled for work and they encouraged me to give it a try. The only problem was that my anxiety had gotten so bad that sometimes I didn't leave my house. I would have food delivered to my house, but only when I knew the person delivering food or if I knew someone else would answer the door for me. I even avoided a certain grocery store for a few years after I was serenaded in a store; I was too embarrassed to go back. Insert a major eye roll here because I'm shaking my head and laughing at myself for that situation.

At this point, I realized that I had two choices. I could stay in the situation I was in and the situation could get worse, or... I could use this situation as a catalyst for change. I chose the latter. Within a month, I applied to agencies, applied for positions, and started working three hours from where I lived. I knew absolutely no one and traveled by myself.

In September of 2018, I took on my first travel contract as a nurse. Choosing to travel has been the best decision I have ever made in my life and probably the second-best thing I've ever done for myself. In December of 2018, I was joking with a friend and talking about my New Year's Resolution. It was to stay single and work on myself. Little did I know how much of a commitment I was making. Ask and you shall receive. I opened myself up to opportunities for growth just by verbalizing that one thing.

When I first started traveling, I was seeking something to replace therapy and ended up getting connected with a Relationship Coach. I remember my thoughts exactly, *"Oh, this will be perfect! I'll figure out how to get a relationship that will actually work."* The truth is that I did form a relationship with someone, but it wasn't exactly what I expected. I've grown to love myself. I enjoy doing things alone. I no longer feel alone when I'm in a crowded room. My anxiety is not cured, but I feel like I can finally breathe without the heaviness on my chest. The absolute best part is that my worth and how much I love myself is no longer dependent on anyone else.

Along with hiring my coach, I started reading many personal development books. My favorite that I suggest to everyone is called, "The Four Agreements" by Don Miguel Ruiz. When it was first suggested to me, the caveat was that it can be a little weird, but if you read it with an open mind you will get what you need from it. While I do not necessarily agree with everything in the book, it has been the most influential book that I have ever read. If you're open minded and need a perspective shift, I highly suggest this book; you will not regret it.

After doing some major work on myself, specifically on my mindset, I still felt like there was one puzzle piece missing. You see, growing up I went to church, but experienced things and really questioned religion because of those things. I wanted to figure out what the heck I believed in. So, I attended and took a few more courses, the most beneficial one was Spirit Junkie Masterclass with Gabby Bernstein. I did a ton of research and talked to a bunch of people. I had truly lost faith in all things, but really I had lost the ability to follow my own gut instincts and intuition. The *"bad feelings"* and *"red flags"* that I overlooked in relationships were my intuition telling me to get the hell out, NOW! After all of this, I have finally gained an unshakable faith in God and the Universe, a relationship that I had once lost completely.

The cold, hard truth is that in the last two plus years, I have learned more than I ever could have imagined. I have grown mentally and emotionally. In all honesty, I do not regret anything that happened to me, because all of those things were happening for me. The Universe has a funny way of helping you learn what you need to. The timing is never a coincidence because there is no such thing as a coincidence. These obstacles are detours in the right direction, and you can always learn something from every situation.

There are still times that I feel insecure. Afraid. Judgmental. Anxious. Angry. Agitated. The beauty of the process is that I can own my flaws and give myself grace, and you can too! There is always room for improvement. I have learned that growth is always just outside my comfort zone. Most importantly, as women, our "magic" is in our power to unapologetically be ourselves without fear.

ABOUT JAYME VELLECA

Jayme was born in Nashua, New Hampshire but was raised in a town a few hours away from Hershey, Pennsylvania. After graduating high school in 2008, she has lived in Bloomsburg and Danville, Pennsylvania. She loves hiking, traveling, cooking, volunteering, listening to music, and singing to her cat- Bobby McGee!

Jayme has a 15-year background in the healthcare industry. Since working as a nurse, she has enjoyed many specialties, but the one she will always be the most passionate about is working in the mental health field in an inpatient unit. This is where she learned how passionate she was about raising awareness about mental health and wellness. She now travels for work and spends her time off exploring and taking in the glorious scenery of whatever new location she has taken a contract in as a nurse.

Jayme is an Intuitive Mindset Coach, motivational speaker, and author. She has been assisting those with managing stress and anxiety officially since 2014, however she remembers coaching friends long before that. She recently launched her newest program called Fear to Freedom, a five-week program that will change your life; the program shares the exact steps she used to release the shackles of anxiety and fear, and accomplish everything she desires. You can join her FREE Facebook community, Managing Stress and Anxiety: Stepping into Your Unapologetic Presence, where she shares tips for managing stress and anxiety, Q & A's every other week, FREE workshops once a month, along with other tools that assist in changing your life.

To connect with Jayme:

jdvelleca2014@gmail.com

Facebook:

https://www.facebook.com/jayme.vellecaarner

Instagram:

https://www.instagram.com/jaymevelleca/

This. Is. Me.

Paula Eberling

*"As a newborn, we enter this world with the purest form of
innocence and vulnerability to the sins of those around us."*
- Paula Eberling

*I am looking at my boss in disbelief. Did he really just tell me
that I overexaggerated on my complaint of sexual harassment? Did
he just say sometimes I get worked up about things that just don't
matter? My voice is shaky and I am struggling to remain calm. My
hands are clammy and my heart is racing. I look down and realize
my fingers are tapping, pulling, and clutching at my pants. I close
my eyes and struggle to find the words to say. I want him to know
that his words sting. Throughout the years, I had become good at
anticipating others' responses and opinions of me. I was an expert
in reading body language and quick in responding to accommodate
the moods, advances, dislikes, or anger that others might have
towards me. I was compliant, agreeable, and giving. Life taught me
how to please others in order to survive. Surviving became a way of*

life for me. My thoughts bring me back to my current situation. My stomach is knotting.

My heart is beating so fast and hard that I can see my blouse moving to the rhythm of my heart. I suddenly realize that this man does not respect my personal space. He does not value me as a female, and most importantly, I have told him that I felt violated only for him to dismiss my concerns. I hear myself say with conviction, "I have survived, I have advocated for thousands of others, but today, I advocate for me. Your good ol' boy system protects the corrupt and dismisses the innocent. What has happened is not okay. I am not okay with this." His smirk told me that he did not hold any value for the words I had just spoken. As I absorb the coldness around me, I thank him for his time and exit his office. I feel like a caged lion: full of fear and rage. I felt my chest tightening and knew that the tears would soon follow. I couldn't let anyone see my weakness.

I get in my car and drive to the first place I feel safe. I park my car outside my husband's work. I can't go in. I am embarrassed that I had let this happen. I feel safe just knowing he is close by. I turn the volume up on the radio in hopes that the sound will drown out my racking sobs. The emotions, the heartaches, the years of pain... they all flood me to the very depths of my soul. What is wrong with me? Why am I crying uncontrollably? Why do I hurt so much? My body is weighted down with all of the emotions from the past. My head feels heavy as the memories flood into my mind. Growing up in a home where fear was the controlling factor for discipline, I had learned to be soft with my words and become invisible. I lacked social skills, self-esteem, and struggled in school. I was conditioned at a *young age to be submissive. Domestic violence taught me fear, and fear taught me silence. I was the perfect victim.*

Many years prior, my three-year-old frame felt the weight of my secrets. My father made us go into the closet to discipline us. It was dark, cramped and musty. I don't remember what we were being disciplined for, but I knew that we dare not leave the closet. I could hear mom crying and my father screaming. I positioned myself so I could see under the door. I saw mom laying on the floor. I saw her attempts to shield her face and body with her arms. I saw my father hitting her repeatedly with the tracks of my brother's race car track. Mom finally stopped crying and my father opened the closet door and then he proceeded to leave. I remember the taxi ride to take my mom to the hospital. I could see the swelling on her face. Mom quietly cries and never speaks a word until she is in the emergency room.

I heard the doctor say, "Lady, if you don't leave...he's going to kill you."

Domestic violence opened the door for me to endure future violence and even sexual abuse.

He calls me from the bedroom, "Paula, come play house with me." The ringlets in my hair are beginning to dampen, my hands are clammy, and my heart is beating so fast that I can see the hem of my dress bounce with every beat. The tiny white flowers on my red dress were dancing. I could smell his perfume, almost like mommy's perfume, but different. My fingers are tapping, pulling, clutching at the bottom of my dress. I'm a big girl. I'm brave, right? "It's okay," he said, "what a good girl." I close my eyes. I can see mommy cooking, I remember my favorite swing in the park, my friend Molly is there, I can hear my bird singing. Mommy's flowers are so pretty. I love my new tea set. I'm okay. I hear him say it's time to go. I really am okay. I remember that mommy is making me cookies tonight. I love her cookies. I am okay.

My mom divorced my dad when I was three and married again when I turned four. She moved us to another state to start her life over. My stepfather wasn't much different from my father. He was strict and quick with his hand, belt, and the rubber garden hose at times. Mom did her best to support us and worked long hours. Her working brought opportunities for the sins of others. The innocence of being a child created vulnerabilities to becoming the perfect victim over and over again. My abusers were babysitters, family members, and even strangers. At twelve, I became desperate to escape the sexual abuse and ran away for the first time. I was found and placed in a home for wayward youth. This was the first time that I became a trafficking victim. As the new girl, I took the place of another and it was my turn to be given to those that could pay. Nighttime became a routine of my body being used and sold. I told no one.

Shortly after it began, I attempted suicide. After being sent back home, I told my mom that I was staying at a friend's house and left out the details that my friend and her mom were actually gone for a week. I thought that I had the perfect plan. I had taken bottles of pills from her medicine cabinet. I would take all the pills and drink the bottle of vodka I had taken from the liquor cabinet. I was planning my death to escape my life. I wore my favorite pair of jeans, fixed my hair, took my pills and drank the vodka. The chalky bitter taste only validated that I would soon be able to close my eyes and escape this pain. I washed down the pills with as much vodka as I possibly could drink. I felt the sleepiness set in and I felt a lightness about me. I felt as if I were floating. Soon, it would be over.

I woke up. As I opened my eyes, I could see the sun shining through the window. I smelled a foul odor and realized it was the odor of vomit and urine. I started crying and was disappointed in myself. I couldn't even do *this* right. I was unsuccessful in my attempt at death. The worst of it was that no one even knew that I had laid there for three days. I felt alone and defeated.

At fourteen, I decided that if I couldn't successfully commit suicide, I would just run away again. But this time, I would go farther. I felt ashamed that my family had recently found out about the sexual abuse. I wanted to protect my mom from the shame and embarrassment of the trial to come. I was called the town whore and a liar. No one believed me, so why not leave?

I snuck into my little sister's room. She was the light in my life and I was going to miss her dearly. I kissed her on the forehead and whispered to her, "I love you." I looked on her nightstand and saw the nightlight that read, "Now I lay me down to sleep. I pray the Lord my Soul to keep; If I die before I wake, I pray the Lord my Soul to take." I said this prayer with her every night. My heart ached, and I prayed that she would remember me. I left her room and went to my room. I opened my bedroom window and jumped with my bag of clothing and personal items. I started off on my journey and was excited to leave this life behind. I walked in the dark of the night and hitched a ride.

I had traveled over a thousand miles. I met a companion and as before, I was so accustomed to meeting others needs, I soon found myself being sex trafficked to cover food and rent for my companion. My survival skills served me well; I had become complacent in order to survive. Once again, I was a master in my own mind and could close down the world around me. It only hurt for a while. I could see mommy baking, I could smell her flowers and taste her cookies. I was okay. I was fortunate that this chapter in my life only lasted two weeks. I was soon arrested for being a runaway, returned to my home state, and placed in foster care. I told no one my secret of being trafficked.

I was blessed to be placed with a loving family. They were the first to believe me and love me unconditionally. I was welcomed with open arms and this was the beginning of a better life. After two years of living with my foster family, I was released at the age of sixteen. I met my first husband in church and married him at the age of seventeen. I loved him for all the wrong reasons. I wanted to hide. I wanted to escape my former life and start a new life. I thought this would save me. I thought he would save me.

Little did I know that I had to save myself. The marriage didn't save me. For eighteen years, I navigated the chaos of love and marriage. Domestic violence still was a part of my life. My past traumas taught me how to live in the mayhem that became a way of life. Some days were good, other days I slipped into the coping mechanisms I learned as a child. My children were the blessing in life. They gave me the strength to move forward. I know I failed them at times, but my love for them was greater than the love for myself. They were the reason I existed. I ended my marriage thinking that I could find my purpose in life, but it would not be until years later that I would discover my true purpose for being.

Nine years after my divorce, I moved to another town. I worked a couple of jobs before I found my current position. Throughout the years, I had questioned my purpose. I was angry with God. I felt as if I were a yo-yo. I would be lifted up, only to be let down. After the loss of a child, I cursed at God. I asked why. It wasn't until I read the job description for my current position that I realized the why. The position was for a Victim and Witness advocate. Finally, my life made sense. I knew every nook and cranny of being a victim. I had been a runaway, sexually abused, trafficked, raped, beaten, and assaulted in my life. The description resonated with my soul. As I finished reading the description, I knelt and cried out to God. I got it. I had to live with the pain. I had to be the victim. I had to feel it, live it and survive it all. I could then use my pain to help others through the process of surviving to thrive. This. Is. Me.

Hearing my boss' words dug deep. I felt unsupported, not valued, and not believable. I needed to hear him dismiss me, I needed to see his true character, and I needed to feel the pain and to recognize the purpose.

The tears stopped flowing. I looked into the mirror. My eyes were swollen and red. Mascara stains trickling down my face. I was a freaking mess. I rested my head on the steering wheel in hopes of gathering my thoughts. I could feel the sun shining through the window. I felt the warmth and started to relax. I felt my mother's presence and I heard her voice whispering in my ear: "Go get 'em, give 'em hell." The feelings of emptiness turned into anger, and then anger turned into hope. I found myself yelling out loud, "That's it, I'm not doing this. I'm not going to let them silence me. You got this. YOU GOT THIS. I know what I have to do."

Hearing my boss' words brought clarity and purpose to my life. I will no longer be a victim. This would be the last time that I would tuck my head in shame and the last time that I would be afraid of my story. He didn't know it yet, but he opened the floodgates.

Today, complacency no longer exists for me. I see myself for the first time. Smiling, I realize I am that person to bring change. My voice can advocate for the three-year-old "Paulas" of the world, my mother, the women that carry secrets of sexual abuse, domestic violence, trafficking... they now have a sister survivor who will carry their voices. It's time to challenge the status quo. I start my car up and exit the parking lot of my husband's work. I drive away knowing that my hardships have blossomed into my greatest strengths. Shame and secrets no longer hold me hostage. This survivor wears her battle scars proudly.

Today, I fight the battle for truth and justice. My hope is that I can make a difference and give others like me the courage to begin the healing process.

It's time to share.

It's time to empower others to find their voice.

Together, we can find the beauty in our pain.

To my surviving sisters, I got you.

Together, we will survive to thrive.

ABOUT PAULA EBERLING

Paula is a wife, mother and advocate for victims of crime. Her passion is empowering women to heal from trauma and self-doubt and become all that they were meant to be.

Paula has served as the Director of the Seventh Judicial Victim Witness Program for eleven years and has 23 years' experience as a victim's advocate. Her prior work experiences in private law offices and County Attorney offices has helped her identify the gaps and lack of resources available for victims of crime in rural Montana. She passionately advocates for services, resources, awareness and social reform of victims' rights.

Paula's influence has sparked state-wide participation as she coordinates multidisciplinary community response teams to create a cohesive response and support system for victims of crime.

Growing up in rural Montana, Paula experienced and has personally overcome sex-trafficking, child sexual abuse, domestic violence, psychological abuse and sexual assault. Through her healing experience, she has become dedicated to promoting victims' rights, supporting victims and witnesses, and empowering survivors in the aftermath of crime.

Paula is a motivational speaker on topics of surviving trauma by sharing her own stories of abuse and trauma as a child to adulthood. Her experience on both sides and sharing her healing journey makes her an excellent liaison, bridging the gap between victims, advocate, prosecution and the criminal justice system.

Founder & Facilitator of the Eastern Montana Human Trafficking Task Force, Founder of the Survive to Thrive Virtual Support Group, member of the Montana Coalition Against Human Trafficking (MCAHT), Graduate of Leadership Montana & Leadership Montana Master's Class, Program Director of the Seventh Judicial Victim Witness Program, Nationally credentialed as a Crime Victim and Witness Advocate, Graduate of the Victim's Advocate Academy, Certified Trauma Support Specialist, Certified Mediator, Facilitator of training's on; human trafficking, victim services, advocacy, surviving trauma.

You can connect with Paula on the following sites:

Survive to Thrive Group

https://www.facebook.com/groups/400682674166684

Seventh Judicial Victim & Witness Program

https://www.facebook.com/7th-Judicial-VictimWitness-Program-778009192241096

Eastern Montana Human Trafficking Task Force

https://www.facebook.com/Eastern-Montana-Human-Trafficking-Task-Force-115958256478158

Eberling Coaching, Mediation and Counseling Services

https://www.facebook.com/Paula-Eberling-Eberling-Mediation-Coaching-Counseling-Services-108344274100804

Paula Eberling Facebook

https://www.facebook.com/lovinglife2day/

My Past Did Not Define My Future: My Path to Healing

Rose Davidson

I STARED OUT THE WINDOW IN MY BEDROOM AND TRIED TO think of a time when I was happy. Nothing immediately came to mind. My thoughts travelled back through my memories, even back to my early childhood. Surely, I must have been happy then. I was sixteen years old and felt old beyond my years. Life had not been kind. There were no happy memories for me to pull from.

My first memory of pain was receiving a beating when I was about eighteen months old. I remember that I slept in the same room as my parents and was a thumb sucker. My father spanked and shook me for what seemed forever. I recall him telling my mother, very angrily, that in the morning my thumbs were to be covered so I could not suck them. Of course, my mother obliged.

I must have gotten better at sucking my thumb because I sucked my thumb in bed, secretly, until I was about ten years old. Then, the "nose eating monster" came.

At the time, I didn't know I was hearing my heartbeat in my ears. The nose biter had pointy ears and a pig nose. If I didn't hide my face under the covers, he would bite my nose off. I can still see him today.

I could never remember a time when my father was not angry in those early days.

It was the summer of 1969. Man had landed on the moon. I had won a night at the local radio station with my favorite DJ. I thought he was the most handsome man I had ever seen. The summer holidays came and all too quickly, they were gone. It was back to school, which meant new friends to meet, a new grade, and a new teacher. All too soon it would be Halloween, Thanksgiving, my tenth birthday, and then Christmas: all the excitement and adventure that a young girl could hope for.

The snow had started early that year, which meant my father was coming home sooner than expected. This meant that he would be home for a longer period of time. These things were only discussed between mum and dad, so I was really none the wiser.

At first, his game was fun. He and I snuggled under a blanket in the loungeroom on a Sunday night. He would kiss me, stick his tongue in my mouth, and touch me in places that brought about these delicious feelings. I didn't understand them. I just knew that I didn't want him to stop. Then, he decided that we would do this on a Sunday morning in the privacy of his bedroom. Little did I know what was to come.

It's 1971. It was Sunday morning again and time for me to go into my parents' room and crawl into bed with dad while mum was cooking breakfast. In the beginning, this weekend ritual was fun. I felt loved. I felt special. Now…I just felt anxiety.

No one in our immediate family ever said "no" to my father, mainly for fear that they would receive a back-handed hit or worse: the silent treatment. So, I was a dutiful daughter and did as I was told.

I remember him telling me that all fathers love their daughters like he loves me. Of course, it had to be true because he had said it. I was sworn to secrecy until I was sixteen.

I soon became tired of the game and of him. I wanted to spend my time with boys my own age and let them do to me what my father did. After all, I was almost twelve and very grown up!

It's July 1972. WOW!! We were going on a holiday– to Germany! We were going to meet my father's family! We were all extremely excited!

It wasn't much fun, though. The only place we went sight-seeing was in Brandenburg, where my father's aunt lived. When we weren't on a train, we were walking and toting our suitcases, which were very heavy. The highlight of my holiday was meeting Peter. I was in love.

What also wasn't fun were the nights. The four of us: Mum, my brother, my father, and me mostly slept together in the one feather bed. I always had to sleep next to my father. I often asked mum if she and I could swap places, but it never happened.

Our six-week journey came to an end and we headed home to Canada. It soon became apparent after we got home from our trip that I didn't have any friends. No one asked me to hang out with them and I was never invited over to anyone's house. If I did venture out to visit them, I was either ignored or they were too busy to be with me.

The next thing I know, we are moving to Australia!

It is now September 1972.

Our move to Australia was spent with me finding excuses to stay away from my father. In Fiji, it was easy. In Hawaii, not so much. There were times that I had to cringe through another session of "loving."

I was emotionally, physically, and psychologically abused by my father as far back as I can remember. Many times, I went to school with a black eye or a bruised butt.

Back in the day, it was never acted upon, so the abuse continued. I lost my virginity to my father at the age of twelve in our caravan, in a caravan park in the Blue Mountains of New South Wales, a state in Australia.

One night after I had attended a high school dance, he picked me up. I sat in the back seat thinking that I would be safe and pretended to fall asleep. He stopped the car somewhere on the way home and opened the back door to the car. He pulled down my panties and raped me. I was humiliated.

I suffered through indignity, heartache and my own major anger issues.

Anger at him.

Unknowingly angry with my mother (this didn't stop until I was fifty-nine).

Anger at myself.

Anger at the world.

I didn't know that I was angry. I just thought I had a bad temper.

The anger with my mother stems from the fact that she was never there for me. She had been seeking my counsel since I was six years old. When I finally confided in her at thirteen about what my father was doing, she didn't do much of anything.

There was that one time, that my father had an industrial accident and it looked like he was going to die. We went to the police to report the abuse. As soon as my father started to recover, she made me recant my statement. I was not happy! I think that's when the anger towards her started to fester like a thorn in my side.

My father recovered from his accident and the abuse continued in ways that I dare not mention. My mother would even get out of the marital bed to sleep in my bed every Saturday night so that I could get into theirs. Oh, how I came to hate those nights.

The sexual abuse by my father stopped when I ran away at the age of fourteen. Little did I know that I was jumping from the fat to the fire. The man I ran away with, although not sexually abusive, was emotionally and psychologically abusive.

I was arrested for being a minor in danger and spent time in a remand centre. While I was there, my mother slept with my boyfriend. Just another hurtful thing my mother subjected me to. In 1974 I had to go to court, and that was a whole new kettle of fish. The process was scary and as a traumatized teen who was not "worldly," I had no idea what was happening. It turned out that the jury believed me, and my father was sentenced to five years in jail.

I finally left the man who I thought was my saviour. As an already traumatized and vulnerable teen, I found it hard to cope. I drifted from one bad relationship to another. Some one-night stands, some not. I was still enduring the emotional and psychological abuse I thought I had left behind.

I went through some serious self-harming behaviour... all the while seeking out the love, acknowledgement, and protection I so badly craved. The angriness inside me continued. I tried to bury it down deep inside, but sometimes it all got too much; it would come spewing out like lava from a volcano.

I went to my father's funeral in 1987. I guess I went to make sure that he was dead. I screamed out in anguish as his coffin was rolled behind the curtain because I never got the answer to the question I was seeking: "Why?" Now, I would never know. That is something that I have had to comes to term with.

In my fifties, I decided to do something about my depression. I had been floating in this deep down, buried bubble of self-loathing anger. Well, mostly anger. Especially towards my mother. Wasn't she supposed to have protected me?

I was finally diagnosed with PTSD, bipolar disorder, and emotional dysfunction disorder. It all stemmed from the years of abuse and trauma that I had endured, which had gone misdiagnosed for so many years.

The abuse had also brought about a chronic pain condition, fibromyalgia, from which I have been suffering from for more than 20 years. This too has been something that I have had to overcome.

The mental health diagnosis put me on the road to recovery, into a place where I could see the wood for the trees. I saw my light at the end of the tunnel.

My story is like so many other abused girls and women out there. Some who have told their stories, some who might not have. All of whom endured things we should not have had to endure. For me, the journey has been long and difficult. I am still working through some of my limiting beliefs and I have still not learned to love myself fully.

When you are constantly criticized and put down, when you are constantly told you are no good, you are stupid, to be more feminine (by my male bosses), you are too fat, you are too loud, you are a loser, you must be perfect (coming second is never good enough), and the list goes on…it can change how you perceive yourself long-term.

Scientific research tells us that our programming is done in the first seven years of life. If the programming is mostly negative, then we as adults will continue to subconsciously believe what we have been programmed to believe as a child.

How have I managed to turn and flip this story around?

It has not been easy.

I've learned to flip the script and change my negative self-talk into positive words, which has been the most challenging for me.

Living a life of gratitude has certainly helped. Being grateful for the little things in life makes for a whole new outlook.

I am still a people pleaser; however, I put it to good use. It's not for my own benefit, it's for those that need my help. I am an advocate against domestic and family violence, and this lights me up.

I strive to not use the words:

- Should

- But

- Can't

- Hate

- Try

- Don't

- Never

Finding and following my spiritual path has been a benefit. I do not believe in God; I do believe, however, that there is a higher being.

Doing things that make ME happy is good for me and for my soul.

For those reading this, I am sorry for the sad journey you may have been on.

Just know that there are others like us.

There are others who have a story to tell.

YOU have a story to tell.

Go and tell it.

It's quite a cleansing experience!

I wrote the following poem to reflect on my life:

TURNING 60

I look back at where I have been, my life, my mistakes, my challenges, my wins, and my losses.

I see the young child - happy, unaware, and unprepared.

I see the young girl - lonely, sad, angry, and hurting.

I see the teenager - rebellious, temperamental, unstable, and head-strong.

I see the young woman- unstable, daring, too trusting, and unchecked.

I see the mid-aged woman - broken and unhealed.

I see the mature woman - finding herself, moving forward, and living life.

And I look again at them all and realize that even through and despite all of this,

I am still here, I am here

I am stronger

I am wiser

I am determined

I am

The challenges and the heartache are just memories, they have made me who I am.

I have overcome them and for that I am proud. I have much to be thankful for.

For I am still here, I am here

I am strong

I am wise

I am determined

I am

[Rose Davidson 2019]

ABOUT ROSE DAVIDSON

Rose is a young at heart, fun-loving woman who is a little on the unconventional side.

She has a "no-nonsense, no fluff" attitude; however, a kind, caring heart, and personality to match. Sounds like a bit of a paradox, but true. Rose has overcome many personal trials in her life and now wants to use her experiences to assist others. In fact, "paying it forward" is one of her many admirable traits.

As an advocate for social justice and an avid campaigner against all forms of abuse, Rose is passionate about equality and justice for all and has volunteered her time at several organizations.

What is particularly near and dear to her is the awareness of domestic and family violence against women, men, and children. Rose is a co-founder and the current president of Healing Through Love, a domestic and family violence awareness initiative which holds an annual Pamper Day event for domestic and family violence survivors.

After a career of more than 35 years in high-level administrative roles in the corporate world, Rose started her business, DOES Biz, in 2015. DOES Biz promotes the administrative services that she could provide female entrepreneurs; however, this did not light her up.

In 2020, Rose pivoted and started her new business, Rose Davidson, as her passion ultimately lies in being visually creative. She now offers services that fulfill this passion to hybrid speakers.

Connect with/Follow Rose:

Email: contact@rose-davidson.com

Website: https://rose-davidson.com

LinkedIn: https://www.linkedin.com/in/rose-davidson

Social Media:

Facebook:

https://www.facebook.com/hybridspeakerexpert

Instagram:

https://www.instagram.com/rosedavidson_
speakersupport/

YouTube:

https://www.youtube.com/channel/
UCJn8KbVcDrbDokFYFGWHtIw

Her podcast 'Talking with the Experts' is about all things business by business owners for business owners is available on:

SoundCloud:

https://soundcloud.com/rose-davidson-76913781

iTunes:

https://podcasts.apple.com/ca/podcast/talking-with-the-experts/id1534682121

Spotify:

https://open.spotify.com/
show/37fmxJuXiAvIzQdCXxhGCP/

As with Language, So with Life

Mistie S. Rose

Have you ever heard that saying, "Why do bad things happen to good people?" Well that's me, I am "those good people." I also go by, "I was minding my own business" and "sure didn't see that one coming." Informally, I go by Mistie and this is a story about the day that forever changed my life. I share this story not for pity, but for empowerment. I cannot tell you what it means for me to be able to share my worth with you, as it is something I did not have at one point in my life.

I can remember January 17, 1998 as though it were this very morning. Twenty-two actual years have passed and without even trying, I can recall every single second of that entire day. I was twelve years old and about to turn thirteen in just four short days. I was at my friend Megan's (I'll call her Megan for anonymity) house for a play date arranged for my birthday. I called my mother and asked, begged rather, to stay the night with Megan. My mother hesitated, then told me to go outside and look around. She asked me if I felt safe. I told her I did, even though deep down inside I didn't. I was in a part of town I didn't know, in a trailer park and in a level of poverty I had not known. I didn't even know what street I was on. All I knew was that Megan was one bad ass chick: the girl everyone looked to for honest thoughts and who feared nothing. She didn't care about other people judging her and honestly, I was with someone I thought wanted to hang out with me. I had a lot of trouble making friends all the way until college. For these reasons alone, I decided I was safe. Yet the next twelve hours would change me to the core of my being. I just didn't know it yet.

The night was cold, and we took a brisk walk in the dark. I wore a borrowed yellow coat to stay warm. So, we walked. It was just the two of us, and Megan the cool girl pulled out an actual cigarette. My dad smoked. I only spent my summers up to that point with my dad. I remember getting ash on me while riding in the back seat of his wife's van. I hated smoking, but I really did want to be cool. This level of cool was just so far out of my league; I started out this school year wearing Winnie the Pooh overalls, so I wasn't a kid that one would expect to be smoking. Anyhow, I tried it, I coughed, she laughed at me, and we walked home.

Megan's dad was younger than my own, shorter than my own, thinner than my own, and I remember he had his tongue pierced (which is something that gets me to this day). He had orange soda waiting for us when we arrived at his trailer. This seemingly innocent beverage, in retrospect, wasn't. Within minutes of drinking all of her soda, Megan said she had to lie down and that she wasn't feeling well. I hadn't had anything to drink. Megan lay there on the futon of a one-bedroom trailer, asleep and unrousable. This did not bother her father whatsoever. He sat cross-legged on the floor and told me to sit in front of him the same way. I reluctantly did. I may have neglected to mention my level of pleasing people was high at that time. I had an inability to say no to nearly everyone, especially adults. So, I nervously sat down in front of him, cross-legged, still in my borrowed yellow coat. I was shaking with nervousness. Whatever was about to happen, my body already knew was going to be uncomfortable. What comes next is hard for me to say, but needs to be heard.

This man's name is Jeff. He is still alive and still lives in my town. He asked me if I wanted a drink. I took a small sip and thanked him. I started to feel woozy immediately. I tried to blink several times and snap out of it. What he asked me next was confusing. He said, "How far do your parents let you shave?" I answered him honestly, "My mother lets me shave up to my knee." He replied, "Have you ever kissed someone with a tongue piercing?" Again, I answered him honestly, "I've never kissed anyone." He showed me his piercing and asked me if I wanted to touch it. I didn't. I sat there in bewilderment and desperately wanted to leave. He then said, "Do you want to kiss me?" I quietly said, "No, thank you" and I leaned backwards. He told me that it was okay. Things would be okay. He got into a cupboard and got out something I had never seen before but that I now know was crystal meth. He offered it to me. I quietly declined. The odd thing was that every time I said no, even as polite as I could, I felt a twinge of guilt. With every "no" the guilt grew thicker. That's the only way I can explain it. Jeff sat in front of me, took several hits from a pipe, then put it away and resumed his cross-legged position.

He looked at me and I tried to look down. I was wearing mostly black shoes called "Pro Wings" which was an off-brand with a white sole. Minutes passed and then it hit me. Literally. A glass jar to the side of the head. I had no idea what had happened. It took a few moments to process it. I saw the jar on the floor. I was hit with a wave of pain unlike any I had ever experienced before and I lay on my side in the fetal position with hot fluid pouring into my hand. To say I was confused would be an understatement. I was crying, as is any normal child's reaction to being hit, which made him angry. He stood up and yelled at me to stop crying and to quiet down. Then he kicked me in the stomach as though that would do the trick. He firmly told me to sit back down the way I was. Tears streamed down my face and I did as I was told. He told me to look at him.

Softly, he told me that wouldn't have happened if I had just gone to sleep. I spit out a hurried reply, "I will go to sleep right now." He stated, "Now it's too late." He softly touched my knee and put his hand behind my head and pulled my face to his. Here it was, my first kiss. A thirty-something drugged out guy. Great.

He kissed me; I didn't move. He didn't like that. I made him angry again. He proceeded to put my arms on his shoulders and he told me to keep them there. He put his arms on the small of my back and kissed me again. Once more I froze, and he pushed me back in frustration with a grunt. I hit my head on the floor. I was terrified. I knew I needed to make him calm down, but I had no idea how. I didn't know what I was doing. I apologized over and over again. He didn't hit me. He told me to stand up and take off my pants. I felt helpless and even worse, I felt hopeless at this point. Once again, I did as I was told. I remember having goosebumps on my legs and my knees were shaking. He told me to take my coat off. I started crying again. I got kicked in the leg for that; my knee buckled and I fell to the floor. I immediately stood back up and took my coat off. Tears still streamed, but I was able to keep from whimpering somehow.

I was instructed to lay down on my back. Jeff sat down to my left and started what I can only describe as "petting" me. Maybe he was attempting to caress me, but at the time I thought about my cat and was baffled at what he would do next. Hitting me? Then petting me? I didn't understand. I still don't. I didn't know what was about to happen. I didn't know about sex. I didn't know about rape. All I knew about boy parts was what school had taught me in fifth grade. He took off my underwear and got on top of me. He took his hand, pressing it over my mouth, and warned, "If you make any sound at all, I WILL kill you. Do you understand?" I did my best to nod "yes."

What followed was the most searing, tearing pain as he entered me; I wanted to scream. I wanted my mom. I wanted my brothers. They always made me feel safe. What I can recall from there is weird to me. I memorized the intricate wood pattern on the cupboard doors closest to me. I could draw them for you, some faux filigree pattern that looked too fancy for the rest of the trailer. I counted seventy-two ceiling tiles all with gray flecks in them. I memorized every detail of the house I could see. His bedding: a loud purple 80's pattern with large shapes. The entire layout of the house. The orange carpets. I saw blood on the jar I was hit with and connected the hot fluid I was holding earlier to blood (the police later called this "disassociation" when I gave them every detail I could). My hair was still wet with it . Some unknown amount of time later, he got up and told me to stay down. Metallica was playing on repeat. I know every song on the Reload album and it is still a trigger for me. I was awake all night from what I remember. I watched the clock and finally at 5:30, I got up to use the bathroom. This woke Jeff. He asked, "What are you doing up?" I lied and told him, "I have church at 6:30 and I need to get home." Oddly, this was fine by him. We got in his car and he took me home.

As if this all wasn't confusing enough, the strangest thing happened when he dropped me off. There I was, in the driveway of my house and this adult man said to me, "I had a really nice time, call me and we'll do that again." He wrote his phone number down. I nodded in agreement and got out of the car. I didn't have a key to my house so I knocked on the door and my brother promptly answered it, which was exceptionally odd given the time of morning. The door flew open and I heard a loud, "What the hell happened to you?!" I said, "I got in a fight with Megan and I don't want to talk about it." Assuming my dark brown hair must have disguised the blood somewhat, he didn't notice anything too strange and replied, "Whatever, loser." I walked immediately to the bathroom, took my clothes off and showered until the water ran cold. I couldn't stand it. It hadn't worked, I still felt dirty. I went to my room, put on the biggest clothes I had, and crawled into bed where I stayed all day and all night.

Morning came and somehow, I was supposed to go to school. Somehow, I was supposed to go out into the world again. Somehow, I was supposed to see Megan. I don't know how I did it, but because there was no one there to ask if I could stay home, I felt as though I had to go. So, I did.

I had no idea the gravity of the situation at the time. How it would shape me and haunt me, even. I had no idea what was really stolen from me until I grew up. I felt like the foundation had come out from under me. I had to find who I was and at this point, I had no inkling of who that was or who I would become.

When my mom found out what had happened to me, I remember she came home from work in the middle of the day crying. She then told me a story I'd never forget. Something I never knew about her: her own horrible trauma. It made me wonder how she seemed to be so normal when she really wasn't. I set out to find how she fooled the world and how l too could possess this trait. Instead of teaching me how to pretend, she put me in therapy.

Yellow walls, rainbows, and huge stuffed bears are all I remember about those sessions. Oh, and the police. I got to tell strangers about my humiliation and witness their reactions of horror. People now pitied me. I didn't know what I wanted, but I knew it wasn't that. Sadly, the look of pity is the only look I saw for months. I had a rough couple of years after that and honestly, I'm surprised I came out the other side of things seemingly unscathed.

The truth is, if I can, so can you. My breakthrough took a lot of time and came at about twenty-six years old. I sought out counseling and met someone who practiced

Eye Movement Desensitization and Reprocessing psychotherapy treatment or EMDR therapy. I would put on headphones and listen to tones alternate from one ear to the other. I would close my eyes and just listen. Gently, my therapist would ask me questions and I found it easier to give her honest answers without the fear of looking into her eyes. I never again wanted to see the look of pity from another human. I could say whatever I wanted and there was no pity. I cherished that.

The idea behind EMDR is that the alternating eye movements or beats that one hears or sees help to access repressed traumatic events and process them in similar ways as we do in REM sleep. Not only can the traumatized patient access more memories, but new neural pathways can be created in the process. On this particular day it was a normal session; I closed my eyes, tried to align myself with the tones, and I found it relaxed me. My therapist asked me to walk through some parts of the night of my rape. When I finished, she asked me to walk through it again, but this time she let me do and be whatever version of myself I wanted. To the greatest extent of my imagination and to my surprise I was a four-year-old girl, then I was a twenty-five-year-old world-renowned kickboxer, then I was the twelve-year-old again. I got to choose who to be and what to do. If I could go back and change any or all of it what would I do, who would I be? She gave me the gift of freedom.

One of the last EMDR sessions I had associated with this event, I decided the experience would still happen. Only this time, I would fight and I would win. I replayed the parts of this scenario in my brain over and over and over again as truth, until it became nearly that. I chose to fight and I became strong, so strong that I was no longer afraid. So strong that I felt empowerment instead of hurt. So strong that I was able to reclaim my life and stop making choices as a trauma response. I won the fight. In many more sessions, through dealing with all kinds of situations that were uncomfortable, choices I wish I hadn't made, and a lot of hard work coupled with dedication, I found myself. I found hope again. I found that I had worth and I continued through all of the muck and uncomfortable feelings because I am worth the work. That is the biggest lesson I came out with on the other side: I am worth the work.

ABOUT MISTIE S. ROSE

Mistie lives in Boise, Idaho with an exceptional husband and two prodigious children: a daughter and stepson. She has an alacrity for service and volunteers for a local animal rescue as a kitten foster. She has a busy home life and enjoys reading, hiking, and exploring Boise's breathtaking foothills.

Historically a research writer, one can find Mistie's published work on Amazon in "The Other Idahoans", a collaboration piece involving her thesis on the Spanish Influenza of 1918-1919 local to Boise. Over the last decade, she studied primarily at Boise State University where she earned both her undergraduate and graduate degrees in Public Health; she specializes in Public Policy. Her goals are to one day write policy on the state and local levels when her children are older. For now, Mistie is working on her next written work in "They Are Magic" coming out in 2021.

You can find Mistie's other published work on Amazon "The Other Idahoans" ISBN-13 : 978-0990736349

To connect with Mistie you can email her at: mistienellie@gmail.com or find her on Facebook at: https://www.facebook.com/mistie.rose.7

Motherhood and Making it on my Own

Elizabeth Thaxton Fogarty

WE HAD A PERFECT MARRIAGE.

Everyone thought so, even me.

Then, we were getting divorced.

I was thirty-five years old, and I had three boys under the age of three.

My oldest was three, and the twins were two.

I was a stay-at-home mom.

I didn't know what we were fixing to do.

It took two years to get divorced, and I met someone new in the process. We got engaged before the divorce was final and married SOON after it was final. They say hindsight is 20/20, and that's the truest thing I've ever heard. The funny thing about hindsight is that we don't ever know about it until later. It's not something you see up front. The good thing is that you will look back, and when you see what's happened, you are wiser because of it. It's true: all the bad stuff that happens makes you stronger in the future. The marriage wasn't bad, I just wasn't ready.

You just have to keep pressing on.

I never took the time I needed to find myself after losing the most important relationship I had had. Honestly, I didn't think I needed to find anything. This is where hindsight would've come in handy, but once again, I can see where all of this just made me stronger for the journey ahead of me. I don't like this at all. I mean, why can't we prevent some of the bad stuff from happening? Why do we want to even be stronger through the lessons??? The only advice I can EVER offer anyone is to NEVER do what I did. I wish that during all of this, someone would have said, "Elizabeth, just slow down." But the question I have to then ponder is: "Would I have become so strong?" Or would I have listened to them in the first place? So, strong it is for my future.

During the divorce process, a neighbor asked me to go to church with their family, and I agreed. I'm not sure what made me say yes, because church was not what I thought I needed. I had never been to a church that made a difference in my life, but I trusted my friend. She had a happiness that I wanted in my life, so yes was a great answer. During my first marriage (that's still hard to say), we were both Catholic and we attended church maybe twice a year on the "big" holidays: Easter and Christmas. I wonder all the time, what could have been if we had Jesus in our relationship.

This was a Baptist church, and it all struck me as strange because I understood all the pastor said and the messages could easily be applied to my everyday life. What in the world? I kept going to church with them and soon after, I gave my life to Jesus Christ. I'll never forget the unmistakable pull to walk to the front of the church at the invitation. I vividly remember holding on to the pew in front of me thinking, "What is happening to me?" This was the beginning of the change in my life that I didn't know I needed.

I'm sure there are those that don't believe, and if that works for you, great. Honestly, I'm not sure how I made it through the first thirty=five years of my life without Him, nor will I ever let a day go by that I am not thanking Him for all that He has allowed me to have in this life.

Now that you know this, let me backup for a second. I have dreamed of being a mom my whole life. Not a girlfriend, not a wife, just a MOM. Not sure I had everything in the right order, or why I hadn't dreamed of being a wife, but all I can remember is wanting to be a mom. I know I was a great wife, because our life together was basically a dream come true, even though it didn't end well. I was all in with him, and I was all in as a mom. I wasn't all in the second time, and y'all, it makes ALL the difference in how you love. If you can't go all in, don't go.

Two years after I got married, we found out we were pregnant. Ecstatic was an understatement. It was here, and I was ready.

I had a miscarriage. It was devastating. But as we know, life keeps going. And as hard as it was to handle, I knew something better would take its place.

Six months later, I was pregnant again. This time, we were good. I basically started wearing maternity clothes right away because I was so excited. My pregnancy was watched closely, and it was literally a perfect pregnancy. And then, just like I had always imagined, my first child was a great baby. I am not even kidding; Andrew was the best baby. Maybe it was just because I had always wanted to be a mom, but, whatever the case, he was everything I had ever imagined. When Andrew was only six months old, we found out we would be having twins. Funny thing, in all that time that I had talked about being a mom. I ALWAYS said, "I will have a boy, and when he is two years old, I'll have twin girls." Thank God I didn't have girls, but as always, God knows what's best for us before we do. So yep, I was having two more babies.

All of my dreams were coming true; right here and right now. It seemed to be that way for a while. I got to stay at home with all three because the cost of daycare would have been almost as much as I was making working at the bank, so it only made sense to be home with them. Once again, my life seemed more than perfect. I think what happened, and I feel like this happens a lot, is that I must have gotten pretty wrapped up in being a mom. I had three babies under the age of two. I see it happen all the time now with new moms. Perhaps I forgot how to be a wife in the process.

Back to the divorce: I was shook. I had three boys barely out of diapers, no job, a mortgage, and bills I couldn't pay. How could this be happening? What had I done wrong to end up here? I was devastated. It had been the first time in my life that I'd understood what unconditional love had meant, and the first time I wasn't selfish in my life.

The one thing that I had been sure of up to this point was that I had been saved, and peace accompanied that.

Don't get me wrong, everything wasn't easy from this point on. In fact, it was awful for years; but that's how Satan works, right? He wants you to believe that the peace you feel isn't real. Some days it's easier to believe Satan, and that also makes it easier to return to our old ways of thinking. Mindset is real; when you understand it, it can change your life, the same way Jesus does.

I had no idea who I was. My second marriage only proved that I never took time to mourn the marriage that was supposed to be "it" for me, so it was doomed from the beginning. Just for the record, running to the next relationship will not work. I am living proof that you need to take care of yourself before you try and take care of someone else. Plus, the damage it will do to your kids may be more than you'll be able to handle in your future. My belief is that your kids are going to see all that you do, and you don't want them to learn all those mistakes you are going to make along the way. If I could just change one thing, it would be that I'd be stronger alone and raise my kids before getting into another relationship.

I had three boys that were playing three sports year-round. I poured all I could into them because I was very aware of what it was like to have a mom that didn't do that. My mom did not actively participate in any part of my life. I vowed to never let anyone feel the way that she made me feel. I overcompensated. I put the boys' needs way in front of mine to the point I forgot I had any. I am NOT saying that I did it the right way, I am just telling you what worked for me. I knew I didn't want my kids to feel they had been replaced, or that anyone else besides their father was more important. I changed what happened to me, so that the cycle of neglect ended with me.

What I struggled with first, was that I wouldn't be able to provide for them, and in my mind, that meant monetarily. I usually had two jobs at a time, and we had to use food stamps and get free meals at school. Talk about depressing. We had Christmases without a tree, and several years without presents. Turns out, when your kids know that you love them and you are always there for them, it goes a lot further than you could ever imagine. That in itself, that is the ultimate gift.

I went back to college eight years ago in hopes that a degree would help me get a better job. My oldest was also about to be in college, so that was fun. It took six years going to school part-time and waiting tables at night; however, I have two degrees now.

What you don't know when you're going through hard times is that you are going to make it. It won't seem like it, but it's always in you. That's the mindset I was talking about. I didn't believe in myself back then, and now I'm stronger than ever. This is 100% thanks to God. No other way I would've made it this far.

While waiting tables in college, I met a lady who introduced me to a new business opportunity. I had never heard of it before, but she said it had changed her life. I joined her without even trying the products because I just knew if it could change her life, maybe it would change mine too.

It did.

Not only did it change my life, it actually changed my skin, just like it said it would. I found my passion here, and I now want to change someone else's life. I heard it said that an extra $500 a month could save a marriage. Just $500 a month. If I could just help one person, it would be so worth it. It enabled me to have time to volunteer for Mission 22, spreading awareness of the fact that 22 soldiers a day take their own life. I became passionate about this after the boys became Marines.

My sons have been Marines for four years, and in this short period of time they have lost several friends to suicide. It has been heartbreaking to see. These are young people who signed up to serve our country and saw more than they realized they would see. When they come home from being deployed in a war scenario, they aren't prepared to live a civilian life when they return home. As extremely frustrating as it is, the veterans don't get the help they need in a timely manner. The urge to try and make a difference somewhere in my life has always been overwhelming, so I researched until I found M22. I've only been involved with them for two years, but it's been a rewarding and a heartbreaking experience at the same time. It's so worth just the investment of my time.

My boys are men now. My oldest is a youth pastor, and the twins are United States Marines. Two are married.

My greatest fear was that the boys wouldn't know how to love. So, I just loved them constantly, and I believe that is how they learned to take care of their wives. I tried dating, but only let a few meet the boys. There was no need in disappointing them further. My job was to be raising my boys, and no one was going to change that while they were still at home. This is just how I did it, and it worked for me.

I have people ask me all the time how I got my kids to be so close to me. Did they ever tell me they hated me? Of course, they did, I'm their mom. I just loved them and I showed up every day. Even when I thought I was failing them, which I felt more often than not, I learned that what they needed from me was to be there for their lives: all in, all the time. When times were tough, we always had each other. When it's good in the tough times, it's better in the good times. The pride that I have in watching my boys lead successful adult lives is not measurable, and it grows more each and every day.

I am 100% sure that God has plans for the rest of my life. My job at this point, is to simply trust Him. I've done it since I was thirty-five , so I've learned that it's the only way to go.

Thank you for taking the time to read my story. I have learned so many things the hard way. I've disappointed many, including myself, but I've also learned a lot; most of those lessons have been life-forming.

ABOUT ELIZABETH
THAXTON FOGARTY

Elizabeth was born and raised in Stone Mountain, Georgia. After finishing high school in 1984, she briefly attended West Georgia College before moving to Dallas, Texas for two years. She returned home where she began her career in banking. She is an avid runner, blue jean and shoe addict, and mom to three very incredible boys, Andrew, and twins Ryan and Stephen. She is currently back in the hometown where the boys were born and raised for twenty years. She has spent her spare time over the last few years watching her eldest's college baseball career, and now his married life as a pastor. She'd also had the opportunity to visit her twins, who are also Marines, and have been stationed on the East coast for four years of their service.

Elizabeth also runs a successful skincare business, which has been the reason that she's been able to enjoy college baseball, and trips to Camp Lejeune. It has also become her passion to help others change their lives as well, whether it's just changing someone's skin, or improving their financial well-being.

To connect with Elizabeth:
etfogarty4@yahoo.com
etfogarty4.myrandf.com
Facebook: https://www.facebook.com/etfogarty

Instagram:
Elizabeth Fogarty's (@etfogarty4)

Prim...

Lisa Lewis

"A warrior focuses on what she is going to,
not what she is going through."
-L.L.

I SPENT THE LAST WEEKS OF SUMMER 2020 IN PAWLEYS Island, surrounded by an ever-evolving scenario of high drama laced with intrigue. It touched my heart and soul as I relaxed with a cup of sweet tea, reminiscing over my past, present, and future.

Today, the beach is peaceful, pristine, and renowned for its surf. I am told that within five miles of the island, there are approximately ten first-rate golf courses and a tennis complex. Fishing is available both in the surf and from the two marsh bridges. On the island, there are three finely made boat launch ramps.

...I do know for sure: Pawleys Island is a family ...where you can delight yourself with crabbing ...dock, shelling, biking, canoeing, or kayaking. The ...biance, like myself, is laid-back. As safe and socially ...istant as possible, I take a leisurely afternoon nap. Once I awake, I call home to check on my eleven-year-old son, Jack Elliott Lewis. He answers, and I proceed to ask him about his day and his studies. You see, as a mum, I have decided to homeschool him; he is delighted with that choice.

Even though I've chosen to pursue my journey as a budding entrepreneur who travels, my goals mostly involve maintaining normalcy and stability for my son. How does one stay true to their motto: "Faith first, family second, career third"? It takes one important caveat: integrity.

I am a strong believer that we are put on this Earth to serve Jesus and to spread the good news of His Word. I have always known about Him; however, I did not fully understand what being a Christian meant until my adulthood. I realized that I wanted to know more about Him and how to live a Christian lifestyle. I've since spent a lot of my time forming my own beliefs about Him. Once I realized how lost I was, and now that I have found Him, I shall never stray again.

It took me a while to understand, "God is within her; she will not fail." Then it finally struck me: if I trust in the Lord with all of my heart, He will lead me to be successful.

This isn't just true for me, it's true for anyone who puts their faith in Him.

We have all been through obstacles where we have struggled so much that we feel like there's no end to the road of failures. I know I've felt this way plenty of times. However, I have to stop and take a few steps back as I ponder His promise: "When you go through deep waters, I will be with you." Then I realize, He is right here fighting the battles with me. I am not alone. You are not alone.

"So, do not fear, for I am with you; do not be dismayed, for I am your God. I will strengthen you and help you; I will up hold you with my righteous right hand." To me, this means do not be afraid, for God is with us. Do not be discouraged, for we have a righteous God, one whom will strengthen us and help us to find our way. God is so powerful that He will lift us up with his victorious hands.

As a surfer passes by, I catch myself reflecting on, "She is far more precious than jewels." I adore this verse because it conveys just how valuable we are to Christ. It took me awhile to fully understand it because I did not think of myself as highly as He thinks of me. By his grace, my mindset shifted completely. Not only do I focus on learning and growing, but I started to realize how beautiful I was in His sight.

A friendly and well-mannered chocolate cocker spaniel is licking my cheeks at this point. I smile. I am caught reflecting on, "Faith can move mountains." Imagine all the good we can do in this universe if people would live as Jesus did. My faith is so powerful and spreading that faith can make a huge impact. I share it weekly on my hourly Apple Podcast titled, "The Lisa Lewis Show." The power of our Creator is so supernatural and getting to experience His grace is beyond magic. I shall never take it for granted. If your beliefs are strong enough, you can accomplish anything. What I have grown to learn is: the power of my faith allows me to do all things through Christ. He gives me the strength, wisdom, joy, peace, and discernment to push towards excellence. Therefore, *She Is Magic!*

From my viewpoint, you can be a mum and live your wildest dreams before your children head off to university. I would not be who I am today without the unconditional love and steady guidance of my own mother, Jeanette McCarter Elliott. Her boundless love gave me the confidence to venture out into the world, while never allowing my feet to get too far off the ground. In this same manner, I guide my own children. With an eleven-year-old still at home, I've decided to continue my adventurous journey as an entrepreneur that travels.

For me, this was a turning point. I would need a village. One that included mentors, nannies, teachers, doctors, and lawyers, just to name a few. This village apparatus exists exclusively to support my eleven-year-old son, Jack. Knowing that prejudgment of my choices will sometimes be intensified as I continue to pursue my God-given purpose of mentoring women, we agreed as a family that I would need help. You need to be supported like the contributor you are. This enables me to continue to serve in a massive way.

One of the many things we did this year as a family was to design a garden. It's a symbol of nutrition and a healthy way of living. Jack and I are able to root around in the soil and get our hands dirty. We enjoyed this sacred time together as mother and son. My prayer is that he too will make this a tradition once he has his own family.

This year, my parenting resolution is to be a better parent, and that will have a profound effect on my entire family and our legacy. I show my son that he is loved by setting boundaries. Children crave limits, which help them understand and operate in an uncertain world. This allows your children to explore and discover their passions just as my son does, safely.

Giving a child responsibility, as I have for Jack, is good for their self-esteem (and your sanity!). When they are developmentally capable of putting toys away, dressing themselves, or making their bed, let them. Your child's mission in life is to gain independence. Do not clip your child's wings.

When you lovingly acknowledge, as I do, your child's minor frustrations without immediately rushing to save them, it helps them understand and operate in an uncertain world. From that understanding, you teach them self-reliance and see a resilience that I get to witness in my son. I've learned to not fix everything; I give Jack a chance to find his own solutions.

As I notice my son doing something helpful or acting with integrity, I let him know how it makes me feel. It's a great way to reinforce good behavior so he's more likely to keep doing it. Instead of me simply saying, "you're great" I try to be specific about what my child did to receive the positive feedback. My advice: give appropriate praise.

No one knows their child better than you as a parent. Follow your instincts when it comes to their health and well-being. If you think something is wrong, chances are... you are right. I've learned to trust my mum's gut, always.

I resist the urge to take on extra obligations or become the "volunteer queen" at my son's school. I will never regret spending more time with my child; I've learned to just say no. For the sake of my son in particular, we have to find creative ways to have fun during this unprecedented time.

My parenting style has churned through the seasons, teaching each of us new things. We never allow our son to be rude or say hurtful words to us as parents or anyone else. If he does, we tell him firmly that we will not tolerate any form of disrespect. We've also passed along our parenting plan to others involved in our son's life. Mobilize the other caregivers in your child's life: your spouse, grandparents, nannies, or daycare workers to get them to help reinforce the values and the behavior you want to instill. For us, this includes everything from saying thank you and pardon me, to acting with integrity at all times.

My early victories in life were a product of the consistent love and high standards with which I was surrounded with as a child, both at home and at school. It was this insight that drove my need to be a productive parent. I want to encourage children like Jack to strive for college and once there, to see it through. I feel that in the coming years, a college education such as the Massachusetts Institute of Technology can only become more essential for young folks entering a global career market.

I've been extremely blessed to have parents, extended family, and mentors who've encouraged me with a consistent, simple message: you matter. As an adult, I am humbled to pass these words on to a new generation.

As I sit on the porch of one of the oldest summer locations on the East Coast, better known as the Town of Pawleys Island, South Carolina, it reminds me of how blessed I am to be a productive and resourceful entrepreneur. I've been able to relax on the beach, sit on sand dunes, visit Brookgreen Gardens, and admire the lovely people that I've met on this journey. All the while I have still been able to work as an author and a skincare consultant.

The cosmetics industry is growing at a rapid speed. With the rise in demand for organic products and growing interest in sustainability, many entrepreneurs are seeing new opportunities in the beauty space. The demand for all types of cosmetic products is ever increasing from varied selections of the population. The demand for premium cosmetics is expanding everywhere, including the middle classes of developing countries. The cosmetics industry includes a vast array of businesses such as anti-aging clinics, aromatherapy, beauty salons, beauty spas, cosmetics stores, hair salons, and even makeup artists. The affiliation that I joined allows me to put "Faith first, family second, career third."

With my marketing skills and being people savvy, it allows me to have a lucrative business. You can too! I sincerely value my consultants and know that "my team members are my greatest asset." I am always proud to add next-level achievers to my productive team. We are called, "Leading Ladies of Mary Kay." If you are planning to start a new home-based business, there is an immense scope for growth; I'd love to connect with you.

According to my research, the U.S. cosmetics market is estimated to have generated a revenue close to $62 billion in 2016. The global cosmetic market is expected to garner $429.8 billion by 2022. Such statistics clearly reveal that there is plenty of business opportunities in this industry. This also shows that you and I can start making profits in this field.

When the status quo won't do anymore, I have found some platinum nuggets that I want to share with you. They will help you take your entrepreneurship to the next level. Fortunately, there are some ways to take your home-based business to new levels without compromising the integrity or profitability of your business.

1) Focus on your product or service and then market it, sell it, and promote it. Do everything you can to increase sales.

2) Find ways to increase sales to your existing customers. It's a lot more effective than finding new ones.

3) Create a website to advertise your company or to sell products online, as I do over at marykay.com/LisaLewis. Thanks to the internet, it's no longer necessary to open a store to reach retail customers.

4) Target other markets. If you sell to working mums, maybe your product will work for stay-at-home mums too, like mine does. While I still want to run my business from home, this has allowed me to pursue new opportunities and network with other professionals.

In my life and as a child, being a part of the 1% was something that was aspirational; now as a *Princess Warrior*, it is an obtainable reality. I petition every reader to take massive action in order to cure the false evidence appearing real. And believe that…She Is Magic, Always!

Dedication:

My mother, for she showed me how to think for myself and how to always show up on time. I use my voice to dedicate this chapter to the lovely, God-fearing woman, known as Jeanette McCarter Elliott. I love you forever.

ABOUT LISA LEWIS

Lisa Lewis is a Mum, the Executive Producer & Founder at Lisa Lewis Company (a media & business coaching firm) and a proud Skincare Specialist at Leading Ladies of Mary Kay. She combines what she has learned from her decade-plus of experience and what she has learned from some of the most iconic teachers on the planet including Les Brown, Tony Robbins, Oscar Elliott, and even Sarah, Duchess of York in an effort to build business strategies that cultivate a culture of love, kindness, and success. She knows the importance of building a business, as well as making self-care a priority in order to have optimal success in business and in life. Lisa understands that business coaching is a great responsibility that can be achieved with one-to-one coaching or through group coaching via Zoom, Skype, conference calls, live events, and VIP days where she travels to your city and spends up to seven hours with one-on-one customized coaching.

Lisa's firm works globally to empower high-level entrepreneurs to transform their businesses and lives by providing support, a sense of emotional awareness, steps to navigate challenges with confidence, and the foundation to build not only a business, but a legacy.

When she is not coaching high energy clients, she is hosting The Lisa Lewis Show on Apple Podcasts, engaging with dynamic people in The Game Changers Circle, volunteering in her community, and is always evolving and contributing as a game-changer, all while raising her brilliant 11-year-old son.

Here's where you can connect with Lisa:

www.marykay.com/LisaLewis

Reclaiming My Magic

Stephanie Norman

I T WAS A BEAUTIFUL SPRING DAY IN APRIL AND THE SUN was shining. I was wearing a sundress, which I loved. My sister had a boyfriend who was in the Navy and he was here visiting. He had brought a friend with him and it was suggested that I go out with them to meet this friend. This friend was amazing. He was so sweet, caring, and hilarious. He seemed to really like me, and he also respected me. We hit it off right away. Shortly after we met, my new love had to go out to sea to practice drills on the aircraft carrier. He would be away for six weeks, and while he was gone we talked on the phone every day. My new love also sent me a bouquet of flowers every Sunday with a sweet message attached.

While he was out to sea, his ship was to dock in San Diego, and they were going to stay docked for a week or so. He flew me to San Diego, and we had an amazing time touring the city, doing things on base, and just having the best time with each other. We spent a lot of time with his brother and sister-in-law. We seemed to have a great bond forming.

We got married three months after we began dating and I was so excited. After we got married, my husband got orders to move stations, and he was assigned to San Diego. We packed up all of our stuff and moved a thousand miles from home. Just three weeks after getting married, I got pregnant. We had the life I had always dreamt of. I was a stay-at-home mom,, and I had a husband who provided for me. We were able to take trips home and had everything we needed.

Fast forward a few years and two more kids…things weren't the paradise that they once were. I was quite homesick in San Diego, so my husband got out of the military and we moved back home. We were married for eight years and it was very mentally challenging for me to endure. My husband kept watch over me at all times, driving me to school, waiting in the parking lot for me to be done with school, and driving me to work. He would watch through the window while I was in class and interrogate me about who I was talking to and why. He would ask, "Why were you laughing, what did he say that was so funny?" "Where did you just go? You said you were going to the bathroom, but you went past it." I worked at a hospital about thirty minutes away from where we lived and I worked the night shift. He would put all the kids in the car and drive to the hospital that I worked at to drive around, watch me, and question what I was doing.

If I didn't want to have sex, my husband would wait until I was asleep and would do what he wanted to me while I was asleep. One time I woke up, told him to get off of me, and was met with utter disrespect and downplaying of the situation. I was told that for someone who didn't want to have sex, I sure acted like I wanted it. This happened often and I felt like there was nothing that I could do about it. My husband also had an addictive personality and was reliant on substances to function from day to day.

After being married for eight years, I found myself unable to trust my own mind. I lived in a constant brain fog and my memory was nearly nonexistent. Many times, I found myself driving with no clue where I was going or why I had even left the house. I couldn't remember anything at work, often forgetting tasks that were easy to remember and had been part of my routine for years. Schizophrenia runs in my family. I thought that I had drawn the short straw and that this is just how it would be. I was going to have to quit my job and be dependent on my husband, who had been unable to hold a job for more than a few months. I felt scared, confused, and defeated. I knew that I was meant for more than this; I had such big plans when I was growing up.

One day, it had been particularly hard for me to function and I couldn't figure out what was even going on in my life. I had two kids at school and one at home.

I couldn't remember if I had fed her breakfast, but it was almost lunchtime. She seemed happy, so I guess she wasn't hungry. I didn't know what time the boys were supposed to come home from school, but that was okay because they rode the bus. I was absolutely against this being my new reality. This couldn't be. I am stronger than this. I will not let this be who I am. I decided to look up the symptoms of Schizophrenia, hoping with everything in me that it was something else.

What I found shook me to my core: it was all a product of my environment. There is something called gaslighting and can cause Schizophrenia-like symptoms. It makes the "victim" (I don't consider myself a victim, however this is the best word that I can find) to not trust their own mind because reality has been distorted for so long. When I realized that this was it, this is what was happening to me, I made a conscious effort to try to remember everything that happened and spot inconsistencies in reality versus what I was being told. Pretty much everything that was happening in my life was a distorted reality.

My mom had let me drive her car and I drove myself to school. It was like a breath of fresh air, being by myself. It was a sweet relief to not have to explain every move I made, explain every conversation I had, and why I had chosen that person to talk to. On the way home from school, I called my mom. I admitted to her, "It's gotten bad." I broke down in tears. I didn't want to break my family up, but I knew that my life couldn't go on the way that it was going. I knew that I was meant for something more and I knew that my kids deserved a mother who could function independently. I also couldn't stand the thought of my boys growing up to be men that did this same behavior to their wives; I couldn't imagine my daughter growing up to accept this as enough for her.

I had attempted to leave a few times in the past and it never worked. I was told that he would take the kids and I would never see them again, or that he would kill himself. My husband also reminded me that I had nothing of my own, not even a car. I was also told that I have no career and I would never be able to provide for my kids on my own. I was told that leaving was selfish.

I made the decision to just leave. While he was at work, I sent him a message that we would be gone when he got home from work. I packed some clothes and the kids. We left. We went to my mom's house. This was the scariest moment of my entire life. Not only was I leaving everything that I had and everything that I had worked hard for, but I was tearing my family apart. I knew I was going to have to face the backlash from him for this decision. The verbal berating and belittling were going to be delivered to me. I was about to be made to feel like I was absolutely crazy. Even more so than I already felt.

So, there I was: a single parent with no vehicle, no home, and no career. Luckily, I had a job. Now, I had to figure out how to function independently when I didn't even trust my own mind. My mom graciously let me continue driving her vehicle and took us in. We moved into her house, where I shared a small bedroom and a full-sized bed with three kids. Now I needed to get my shit together and make something out of myself to give my kids a life that they deserved.

I had wanted to be a paramedic since I was in high school. I had even gotten my EMT certification and had taken some classes toward paramedicine. I got a new job at the VA and I went to EMT school. I got my EMT certification and I applied at a few places to work as an EMT with no success. I stumbled across a posting for a reserve EMT at a local ambulance service. I didn't think that I would get hired because this was the service that everyone wanted to work for; I had also been told that they didn't hire EMTs. I was emailed the link to take the test and was offered an interview, which led to being offered a reserve position. As a reserve, I volunteered my time on an ambulance, but in return I got priceless experience with a 911 service.

Then, it was time to go to medic school. I applied and got an interview. One of the interview questions posed to me was, "How do you think that you will be able to complete this program while working two jobs and having full custody of three kids?" This was a nagging thought that I had in the back of my head anyways, but failure wasn't an option for me. I told them that I would do everything that I needed to so that I could pass the program and eventually become a paramedic.

The paramedic program was not easy and was just about two years of non-stop running. I worked two jobs, I volunteered as a reserve, I donated plasma, and I went to school full-time. I worked to pay for daycare and gas. I donated plasma to pay for my kid's school lunches. I spent many weeks with only one day off and some months only having a few days off. My kids probably thought that I had abandoned them, and my family eventually stopped asking me to hang out or do anything with them because I was constantly busy. In the middle of my paramedic program, I was offered a part-time job at the ambulance company that I was volunteering for. This was incredibly exciting news because now I got to get paid for the work that was doing with them. The job offer made me feel so much better about my upcoming internship, because my internship was supposed to be two twenty-four hour shifts a week for ten weeks and no pay. So, at least I would have another way to make a little bit of money.

When I was almost done with the paramedic program and I just had my internship left to do, the ambulance company that I worked for offered me a full-time job, starting with my internship! I sat in my chief's office and I cried when they offered me the full-time job. This was absolutely pivotal in my life. I was almost done with my paramedic program, but it was hard to get hired as a paramedic at a reputable service running 911 calls in my area. It was a divine gift to be given this opportunity, and to be offered to be paid throughout my internship! I got paid for my internship!

It was the most amazing feeling to be able to quit all of my jobs and only work one. No more school, no more donating plasma, no more clinicals; just working two twenty-four hour shifts a week. Now, my next major hurdle was to pass the certifying exam and practical to become a paramedic. When that was done, I felt a huge weight lift off of my chest. I felt free and accomplished. Since I was done with school and had a career, it was time to move out of my mom's house. I moved out with my kids and we moved into a rental.

I have now been with that paramedic company for about five years total, two of them being a paramedic. I support my own household. I take care of my three kids, and I just bought myself a new truck. We are happy, healthy, and we have overcome so much.

I wanted to share my story because I want to empower anybody who may be in the same position that I was in. I don't know what was harder, making the decision to drastically change my situation or putting in the work that put me where I am today. It was all an incredibly humbling experience. I was scared to my absolute core to make the decision to go back to school full-time with three kids, but I did it and I am so happy that I did. Watching the change in myself from the point that I decided to leave my marriage until now is astounding. I have changed for the better in many ways. I wouldn't change what happened because it made me a much better person, and I got three beautiful children out of it.

Just remember:

You are stronger than you think, and you can do whatever you put your mind to.

You deserve to be happy, and nobody is responsible for your happiness other than yourself.

ABOUT STEPHANIE NORMAN

Stephanie Norman was born in Boise, Idaho and raised in Nampa, Idaho. After graduating high school in 2007, she attended one semester of college at Idaho State University in Pocatello, got married, and then lived in San Diego, CA for a year before moving back to Nampa, Idaho in 2009. She is an avid CrossFit lover, free spirit, glitter addict, and mom to three beautiful children Bradley, Brayden, and Chloe. She currently resides in Southwest Idaho with her children and enjoys paddle boarding, camping, and lifting weights in her spare time.

Stephanie is a nationally registered paramedic in her hometown. Stephanie is passionate about nutrition and fitness, and is a dedicated dog mom to two German Shepherds, Duke and Bella. She has helped the community by participating in fundraisers to raise money for the local Boys and Girls Club, and often volunteers in her children's classrooms. Stephanie hopes that her story has will inspire many to handle any situation with grace and love for themselves.

You can connect with Stephanie here:

https://www.facebook.com/StephanieNormanAuthor/

Phoenix Rising

LeeNor Dikel

E ACH AND EVERY ONE OF US HAS A STORY. A JOURNEY AND a purpose and a whole lot of in between. If someone would have told me a year ago that I would be where I am today - *who* I am today, I would have laughed. Today, I still laugh, but with tears of joy and gratitude dancing in my eyes.

Our story physically begins the day we are born, but it *truly* begins the day we are tested. In the years in which I studied at the University of South Florida; I experienced many things. Most of these experiences were wonderful and exciting and empowering. However, there was one thing that left a bitter taste in my mouth for years to come. During my time in college, I was statistically one of every *three* girls that will wind up in an abusive relationship. One that left me a shell of who I was, full of self-doubt, confusion, and a pain that drills down to the bottom of your soul and sits there until you decide to step up, and do something about it.

There were many nights that I cried myself to sleep. Many days that I struggled to get out of bed. Finally, one night, I said, *"enough."* What I once allowed to define my life would no longer hold that power. In *that* moment, I took my power back, and it was in that moment, that my journey truly began.

I once read that in Japan, broken objects, many times, are reconstructed using gold because in this culture the cracks are actually seen to give the objects more character, and worth. Just like how, while we might see ourselves as "broken," we actually only become stronger and more beautiful, even when we might not always feel like it.

In the beginning of my journey, I felt broken. Hopeless. I could throw out a million words to describe the emptiness I felt at the pit of my stomach and the weight at the bottom of my soul, but I think the best one would be "lost." When I first began my journey, there were many moments in which I wanted to give up. I asked myself, I looked up and asked God, *"Why?"*

And then I got my answer.

In my pain, in my confusion, in my hurt and heartbreak, I found my purpose. She snuck up on me like an old friend, tapping me on the back and reminding me that I am not alone. That there is a spark, a flame inside me that never left, only dimmed for a while, and was ready to come back, reignite-light, and shine in all its beautiful glow.

When I was a child, I loved to help people. I was always the person who others would come to for advice, always the little sage. Even if I didn't fully relate to their situation, somehow I always understood people, and the right words would intuitively flow from my lips and touch their soul. This continued throughout high school, and I soon had realized that I had a gift. But college came and I made the "rational" choice to pick a field and study so I could get a good job and be that good citizen everyone wanted me to be. Come sophomore year, I was assigned a mentor from my scholarship program, a beautiful woman who encouraged all of my life-coaching dreams. However, it was not long after I began working with her that I met my ex-partner and I lost sight of my dreams. By the time I gathered the strength to leave, I was already broken down and lost, or so I had thought.

It was in that hopelessness, in my darkest moments that I thought everything was pointless and my spark was forever gone, that I found the smallest bit of hope until I held on so tight and firm that it continued to grow again inside me like a flame. Each nurturing affirmation, meditation, kind word, long walk outside, journal session and yoga class sparked the flames only higher. As I began to regain not only my hope, but my spark, I realized that I had gained much more than I had lost.

I had not only found myself again, but my purpose as well. I had brought myself back from a dark place that, to be honest, in the past part of me doubted that I ever would. I had healed my heart. Through prayer and hard work, I had become rejuvenated. *Reborn.*

I looked back at where I used to be, then observed the place in which I currently was, and for the first time I felt true, deeply rooted respect for myself. And I made myself a promise - that I owed it to the child within me that worked so hard to heal - to go after my dreams with all that I had. So I did. I began to work on myself with everything that I had in me, figuring I had nothing to lose. If I could overcome everything that I did, there is nothing that could stop me from going after anything that I desired - a life of freedom, liberty, touching hearts, and changing the world one soul at a time.

I decided to chase my dreams - even if I was afraid. I started doing more and more things that scared me, until I wasn't scared anymore. I invested time in learning more and more about myself until I had such a clear idea of what I wanted in life that I could talk about it for hours without tiring. I invested in the certificates I needed - to learn what I needed to learn - to be able to dedicate myself to what I love. I started to spend more time doing the things that filled my soul and saying "no" more often to anything that drained me, or that I simply didn't feel aligned with. I invested in my relationships, nurturing friendships with the people who decided to stick around when I needed them the most, and making sure I was always there when they needed me, too. I began to fill my days with my gratitude practice, time with family and phone calls with friends, working on my goals and health, until I became a version of myself that had not only grown and healed in ways she thought impossible, but knew exactly how to help others do the same. I began to think of myself as a garden, and so I cared for myself and all of the beautiful flowers in my life as if I were one.

The healing process is not one size fits all. In fact, for each and every one of us, it can look quite different. While the process itself ebbs and flows in a manner which best fits its guide, there are certain things that all of us need to heal.

When I began the healing process, I couldn't even claim that it was intentional. There was no guidebook or story that I had to follow - instead all of my guidance came from inside. I find that oftentimes our best ideas and strongest moments have a deep link to our darkest experiences. It was from that place in my life where healing became not a choice, but a necessity.

In this section, I want to walk you through the necessary first steps that I took until they become so clear to you, that you can easily replicate them in your own life. Whenever there's something that we don't want to do, but we know is absolutely essential, it is often compared to "ripping off a bandage." In this same way, the process of healing could be easily described. While healing is complex, beautiful and full of twists and turns...there are two very clear points in the process which are evident in almost any person's journey. The before and the after. In this light, I do not refer to the "before you are healed" and "after you are healed" but more so, before you make the decision to heal and the after. Because the first and often the most difficult decision is simply to *begin*.

So how does one do so? It is important to recognize that the root of this fear so often associated with healing, is a deep-rooted resistance of coming face to face with emotions and the inner self. For this same reason, many have claimed that hypnosis or meditation "do not work" because they were facing this same deep-set resistance to allowing these modalities to melt away their inner walls and open the right doors. You see, in our society we *fear* fear. We *fear* emotion. We *fear* anything that will make us appear "weak." For that reason, the first step in the healing journey is to recognize that opening those doors and coming face to face with our demons is actually incredibly *brave*. That *crying* is actually incredibly brave. That *feeling* in a society that advocates for surface level satisfaction and tools that numb rather than open us up...is actually incredibly *brave*.

Allow yourself to feel. Allow yourself to cry. Gently peel away those hardened layers that have formed a protective barrier over the years and whisper to your heart that you are ready. Because you are, and in reading this book, you have taken the first step, so acknowledge yourself for that as well. Now, once you have peeled off the layers and ripped off the bandage, here are a few things you can do:

> *Meditate* - In my healing journey, meditation and mindfulness were absolutely essential and is something that I continue to practice to this day. Meditation allowed me to reach parts of my mind that had previously seemed inaccessible, to speak to my heart, to find peace and greater knowledge in everything that I had and would experience, and to develop an utter sense of gratitude for simply being alive. Meditation allows you to connect to the root of your inner being and grounds you in your truth. In my practice, I would utilize chakra meditations to balance my energies, manifestation meditations to reinforce my dreams in the Universe, gratitude manifestations to develop an infinitely more expansive and optimistic view of the world, and simple mindfulness exercises such as mindfulness of breathing or walking mindfulness to connect with myself and with my truth. To be at peace with the impermanence and ever-changing reality of the world.

Connect with nature - Have you ever noticed the incredible sensation of warm sunlight tickling your back, comforting you, healing you, and filling you with light? Connect with nature. Step outside. In this busy and often hectic world, we find ourselves hunched over the computer, imprinting our eyes with the same images of our Instagram feed or perhaps all the work we have left to do. It wasn't meant to be this way and it doesn't have to be. We are nature and nature is us. The same way our body needs water to fill it up, it needs sunshine to help us glow. Spending at least twenty minutes outside per day has been demonstrated to greatly improve life satisfaction, as sunlight has been proven to reduce stress, boost levels of serotonin in the body and even help us live longer, healthier lives. Spending time in nature heals - it allows us to connect to the world around us as well as to the truest version of ourselves.

Affirmations & Information - Something that really helped me heal from my abuse was knowledge. Apart from the fact that learning can physically heal parts of the brain that were negatively impacted by trauma, it is incredibly empowering to develop a greater understanding of what you experienced and to validate what you are feeling. More so than that, it is important that while you fill yourself with information you also flood your subconscious with the positivity that you so much need in your most vulnerable moments. I once read a quote by Rumi that said, *"The wound is the place where the light enters you."* When we feel our most broken, we are self-perceived to be our most vulnerable, but there's also something pretty damn beautiful about that. We are at the place where we are also the easiest to mold and we now have the chance to do so with all of the positive intentions in the world. So, take this time to educate yourself about what you experienced and whatever you need to heal from. Researching as much as I could about narcissistic abuse was incredibly empowering, allowed me to understand so many things that previously had me tossing and turning night after night, and truly take my power back. Life doesn't come with a manual and especially not for our most difficult moments. So, invest in knowledge. Understand what you went through and why it affected you the way it did. You will find so much strength, power and validation in that knowledge alone. Then educate yourself - on all of the amazing things you can become. Watch videos on things that interest you and learn about all of the amazing opportunities that exist out there now that you have time to focus on yourself. Embrace the fact that you now have the chance to truly thrive; to fall in love with learning about all the beautiful wonders and possibilities this world has to offer. I personally like to listen to positive affirmations every morning as I stretch and work out. If it works for you, write these down and recite them out loud. It is your time to craft your life, to take your power back. Now is your chance to do just that.

Nutrition & Health - Food heals. Water heals. Your diet and the way you treat your body *matters*. One of the most important things that I learned on my healing journey was that feeding my body healthy food was equally as important as flooding my psyche with positive thoughts. I like to start my day with a nourishing combination of protein and fruit right after my work out and make sure I'm eating healthy amounts of nurturing food throughout the day. A good balance of healthy fats and carbs and of course fruits and vegetables is essential to a balanced diet. As well as, drinking at least eight glasses of water a day to boost your immune system, increase energy, flush out toxins, and so much more. I also recommend substituting your second cup of coffee with green tea and consuming at least one detox tea a week. Aside from being nourishing, drinking tea can also be incredibly comforting. This was beneficial for both my body and my mind in the healing journey, and continues to heal my body every day.

Connection - I left this one for last, but it's potentially the most important. When I first came face to face with the reality of my trauma, the first thing I did was isolate myself. It was, in fact, reaching out for support that turned a lot around for me and helped me heal. It's important to remember that not everyone is going to understand you and instead of letting this turn you bitter, hold on tightly to the ones who not only promise to try, but stick around and support you long after you need it. Establishing healthy relationships with other loved ones or even seeking professional help are some of the most healing things you can do, especially after a trauma involving someone you used to deeply trust. Another thing that you should never feel pressured to do, but is likely to help, is speaking your truth. It took me a *very* long time to open up to anyone about what I had been through, but although it came with anxiety at first, it was one of the best decisions I made and one of the most liberating things I could do. There are some misconceptions about speaking your truth. This doesn't have to look like a wide-spread announcement of everything you've experienced, at all. It can simply be opening up to a friend, a coach, a therapist, or even to your journal. Speaking your truth to people you trust and who support you in your journey can be incredibly helpful and often very validating. Activities like journaling can also serve to help you process whatever you are trying to heal from and reach new perspectives that can reinspire hope and even give you purpose.

I healed.

I stretched.

I expanded.

I grew.

What I once saw as my downfall, became one of the best things that could have happened to me, and I knew that the man who had tried to destroy me in some funny way was the reason I knew to grow wings. I could no longer be held down. No longer live as a shell of myself. I knew I was meant for so much more than that. All of us are. We go through situations that change our lives, but one day, the pain fades and we realize that through the ashes we were reborn. It is in that moment that we rise, just like a phoenix from the ashes of who we once were, and the inferno that we once experienced, transforms into the flames of our passion, resilience and spectacular rebirth.

Although I would never wish what I experienced on someone else, I have found grace, and I have found gratitude for my past. Because I know that today, I am a woman that I can be incredibly proud of. Living in her truth, making waves, still learning, and still loving herself every step of the way.

ABOUT LEENOR DIKEL

LeeNor Dikel is an Internationally sought-after Intuitive Guide and Accredited Empowerment Coach. In her practice, she leads ambitious women seeking to overcome subconscious blockages, alleviate stress, and shift into the best version of themselves. She draws upon her expertise in neuro-linguistic programming, hypnosis, and mindfulness, as well as her own extensive experience, in guiding her clients to move from "stuck" to empowered in every aspect of life. LeeNor works with clients to discover their purpose, break free from doubt, tradition, and insecurity, and to go after their crucial goals without fear and hesitation holding them back. Utilizing her 3-Step Strategy For Success, she helps her clients conquer these limiting beliefs, embody self-love, and develop a game-plan that works to cultivate the lifestyle, business, and relationships that bring them joy and allow them to thrive.

LeeNor Dikel is also a published author, speaker, and host. You can explore her other books by checking out her author page on Amazon. Her latest work, The Game-Changer Workbook is a 150-page intensive for women looking to upgrade their lifestyle and go after their dreams. She is the founder of From Striving to Thriving In 90 Days, a program and course that helps individuals around the globe take their life into their own hands and to the next level. She also writes for Thrive Global and Brainz Magazine regularly, and can often be found leading workshops or featured in various podcasts. To be sure you don't miss any of this, you can join her FREE Facebook group for incredible connection and growth at: https://www.facebook.com/groups/abundantbossbabes where she often hosts her free events and gives out exclusive freebies!

You may find more of her work at www.lifewithleenor.com and to connect with LeeNor, you can reach out at:

Email:
leenor@lifewithleenor.com

Facebook:
https://www.facebook.com/lifewithleenor

Instagram:
https://www.instagram.com/lifewithleenor

Kitchen Sink Crisis

Liz Reddick

DECIDE

"It all starts with a decision to be great"
-Brooke Price

IT WAS A TUESDAY MORNING AND I WAS STANDING AT my kitchen sink in a semi-conscious state. I was exhausted, overwhelmed, and being slowly driven crazy by the "PJ Masks" theme song on repeat in my brain. All the "things" were swirling and piling up around me: a messy kitchen, piles of laundry, toys everywhere, and a living room that looked more like a jungle with dragons and wild animals running everywhere. On top of it all, I hadn't showered in days. The only thing I could do was stand there, look out the kitchen window, and cry. I didn't have the energy to move. I didn't have the capacity left in me to cope with the chaos. All I kept thinking was, "Is this it? Now that I'm a mom…these are my days? This is my new reality? My main purpose is now to provide snacks, do laundry, and organize sleep schedules while following around these little humans and picking up after their creative destruction...seriously?" Don't get me wrong, I absolutely adore being a mother. I had just accidently let myself get swallowed up by motherhood.

As I stood there in a bit of a trance, this thought (seemingly out of the blue) popped into my head:

YOU DON'T HAVE TO GIVE UP YOURSELF
TO BE A GOOD MOTHER.

My first response was "Yeah, right. Yes, you do... obviously!" In fact, I think I actually laughed out loud. Seriously, the thought was so ridiculous to me that it was humorous. *Of course,* you give up yourself and your own dreams or desires when you become a mother. There's not enough space for both...right? Isn't that part of the job description? Sacrifice is the name of the game, or at least that's how I was taught. The more you sacrifice, the better parent you are. Isn't that how it goes?

Then it hit me, "IT IS A CHOICE." Loud and clear, it was like I had suddenly been awakened. I was *choosing* to see it this way. What my children need is a mother who feels fulfilled, a mother who's inspired, and who takes the time not only to acknowledge her greatness, but to claim it. They deserve that version of me. *I* deserve that version of me. *That* is what being a great mother looks like.

Well, heck…I'd had it all wrong. I wholeheartedly believed that my sacrifice was noble, that sacrificing my own passions and desires made me a good parent. The truth of the matter is, sacrifice has *nothing* to do with motherhood or being a good parent. Motherhood is about learning, growing, giving, and receiving. It's not about sacrifice. It's *definitely* not about self-abandonment.

That day I brushed myself off, took a shower, and chose to start seeing things from a different perspective. It all started with this simple decision: a choice to take back my control, to step into my power, and to show my children what it looks like to follow your dreams.

Glennon Doyle puts it so perfectly in *Untamed* when she says, "My children don't need me to save them, my children need to watch me save myself."

For me, "saving myself" took the form of me finally using my voice. I acquired a coaching certification, built my consulting company, started a business Instagram account, hosted several workshops, and offered talks to support other mothers. I helped others with the lessons I had gained through my experience of losing myself and finding her again.

Do you know what the best part was? It was my children; it was them watching, learning, and absorbing like little sponges as their mother stepped into her power and paved her own path. They are my driving force, my "why"; *they're* the reason I will continue to reach higher. As a parent, I have committed myself to being an example for my kids. One that teaches them firsthand what it means and looks like to realize your dreams, claim your power, and live a joy-filled, purpose-driven life. I live in the hope that my example will trickle into their precious minds and become the foundation for them to have the confidence to claim their own greatness without hesitation.

So, I will ask you now:

What are you deciding?

Who are you choosing to be?

SHIFT

"The only limits you have are the limits you believe."
-Wayne Dyer

For years, I kept my big dreams of being a coach, an author, and a motivational speaker silenced. Only my closest friends and family knew how deeply committed I was to personal development and the extent in which I enlisted the power of positive thinking. Not to mention, my obsession with the intuitive and cosmic magic of the

Universe (which, for the record, can be found in almost any moment - mundane or spiritual).

But why wasn't I proud of this? Why did I keep this dream hidden? Why did I keep my desires a secret? Well for one thing, it was fear...and the other, self-doubt. They were both keeping me small and keeping me quiet.

I remember one day, while I was chatting with a group of female co-workers, we all started talking about our hobbies and sharing our passions. The women shared their passions that ranged from interior design to holistic nutrition to yoga and more. These were all things which, to my mind at least, seemed to not only be authentic passions but also potential legitimate careers. I remember my thoughts as I sat and listened, "My passion is thinking positively (hmmm...weird!). No one will ever take that career seriously." I spent years pushing this desire down, trying to ignore its light (my light) and trying to tame its fire (such a shameful waste of good energy). If I had only known that it was my own judgment, self-doubt, and fear about the career I dreamed about and my ability to succeed that were keeping me small and keeping me quiet.

Fear and judgment are powerful, especially when the fear is deep within you and the judgment is your own. Deep down, I was the one that thought my dreams were too unrealistic and weird. I was the one that believed that my thoughts, abilities, and desires were no different from anyone else's. *I* was the one that needed to break free from my self-imposed silence, shift my perspective, and speak my truth.

And so...*I started.*

I started by giving myself permission, permission to be proud of my passion. I immersed myself by diving into any content I could find. I left no book, podcast, or teacher in the mindfulness and self-awareness field untouched; I shared and leaned into their knowledge.

I finally got out of my own way. I unequivocally recognized and realized nothing was ever standing in my way except myself. There were no limitations except the ones my mind had created. I decided to make it my intention to shift my limiting beliefs. I decided to make it my mission to believe in my calling.

Limiting beliefs are very sneaky. These self-saboteurs can be so deeply rooted within us that it is hard to recognize their presence. In fact, we often mistaken them for our reality, going about our daily lives accepting them as truth and allowing them to shape our decisions and actions. The truth about these "sneaky little" beliefs is that they don't actually belong to you. You are not being forced or mandated to keep them or act upon them. We have the ability to set them free. We can choose to believe and keep those thoughts or ideas which are more positive, powerful, and empowering instead.

One thing I learned from my coach, Emily King, that never fails and always has the ability to call "BS" on limiting beliefs is to ask yourself this one question: "Who would I be without this thought?"

When she first challenged me with this question, I instantly knew the answer. The thoughts that fed my lack of confidence were enabling me to stay in a comfort zone, allowing me to play small, and keep myself safe. In my mind, it was a reasonable justification. It was a safety blanket that gave me comfort and afforded me an excuse not to seek my truth or embrace my power. But what would I be without this belief? Well, I would be a successful entrepreneur! I would acknowledge my passion and be a confident woman! I would be powerful in my conviction, and certain in my own vision and abilities!

Why do so many of us hold onto such crazy, untrue, and limiting beliefs about ourselves? The way the system truly works is that each of us get to choose our thoughts; they do not get to choose us. We get to choose which thoughts we give power to and in turn, we create our own realities.

I'm making a choice and I'm choosing to send them back: all my wild, false, self-limiting, and inhibiting thoughts about myself, my inabilities, my self-doubt, my lacking, and my unworthiness. They can all go, the whole lot! Who's with me? It's time we all stood up and embraced what we're capable of. Let's shift these limiting beliefs and allow our authentic selves to shine.

You owe it to the world, and you owe it to yourself, to share your gifts, passion, and power. Get out of your own way and decide to rise above. Claim your calling. Anchor yourself deep into knowing that your dreams and desires have been given to you because you *can* achieve them. Your next step is to fuel them with some passion.

Now ask yourself:

What gifts are you hiding within and keeping for yourself?

Psssst…it's time to let those gifts shine!

ACT

"She was never quite ready, but she was brave. And the Universe listens to brave."
-Rebecca Ray

Remember when you were a kid at an amusement park and there was a roller coaster? You may have been one of those kids who wanted to ride it over and over again. Or, maybe you were the one who really wanted to, but couldn't get past the guttural fear. Well, I wasn't either of those kids. I really, genuinely did NOT want to go on that ride (cue horrible memory of vomiting off the side of a full motion roller coaster!).

Regardless of what GOT me on the roller coaster (peer pressure, a need to please, or curiosity) the truth is, it felt amazing getting off that ride. It was almost amazing enough to want to do it again! The "Fear vs. Bravery Ride" works the same in adult life as in childhood. When you take scary steps to becoming your next-level self, you get a rush, and it may just be the unforeseen momentum that will keep you moving forward.

This journey really is a roller coaster. It's a wild ride involving growth, setbacks, learning, and moments of practice, highs, and many, many lows. Everyone's starting point is exactly that: the start! As we keep trying, we move forward: learning, growing, and improving. All amazing stuff, but we had to start the journey.

Here is some sage advice: let it suck! Embrace the terrible. Keep moving forward. Keep trying new things. Keep showing up for yourself and your dreams.

And how do you do that? Get. On. The. Roller coaster!

You must act. Lean in. Make waves. You must do the scary things when they present themselves. Scary sucks! It really does, but the "scary" and "uncomfortable" places are the only route to true self change, growth, and success. So, DO the scary thing. Be brave. Go all in…and hold on. It's going to be a fun ride!

Ask yourself:

What scary thing have you been avoiding?

What scary action step will get you one inch closer to your next-level self?

What can you do today?

RECEIVE

"You can get to where you want to be from where you are- but you must stop spending so much time noticing and talking about what you do not like about where you are."
-**Esther Hicks**

By now, you can probably tell I'm a big fan of this little thing we call the Universe and all its cosmic wonders and gifts. Call it whatever you want: The Universe, God, angels, guides, divine intelligence, consciousness, Love; there are endless versions and truthfully, it doesn't matter. What *does* matter is that you have a relationship to something greater than yourself, and that you believe in a power, a force, a truth…that guides, supports, and works with you.

With belief and trust in this power, you can really step into your own and the ability to be the co-creator of your life, hand in hand with the Universe's divine energy. This is where the big magic happens, real magic! This is you getting into the groove with the Universe and mastering your manifestation abilities.

I joke with my husband that I manifested him into my life (he thinks it was his undeniable charm and good looks that drew me into his world). The truth is, I was working hard to learn the art of manifestation. I figured if I could tap into this divine intelligence (the Universe), then maybe I would have a shot at meeting a decent guy and shot at having the family life I'd always desired and dreamed of. So, I Feng Shui'd the heck out of my house, did visualizations, created vision boards, joined dating sites, and started to just have FUN with my new job, calling the perfect relationship into my life. It was a process, a real journey, and it didn't all magically happen overnight. However, it did happen and I know that my trust in the Universe (matched with the action I was putting into this manifestation exercise) had a LOT to do with the end result: a loving marriage at the core of a flourishing young family.

Here are the manifestation guidelines that I implemented on my journey to find love. I continue to work with these to deepen my understanding and trust within.

1. What you focus on, you create more of.

    Gabby Bernstein teaches that we're constantly manifesting every day, consciously or unconsciously. "You are always a YES for something." She explains that you're either a yes for what you want or a yes for what you *don't* want. Simply put, whatever you're focusing on is what you're attracting more of into your life.

    Stop obsessing over your fears, stop giving energy to the "shouldn't, couldn't, wouldn't, and can't" words dominating your thoughts and driving the feelings connected to them. Now, start focusing on what you *do* want, on what is *already* working and making you feel positive.

    Ask yourself: based on your focus alone, what are you saying YES to?

2. How does it feel, not how does it look.

    We manifest and create based on how we FEEL. Our emotions and energy act like a magnet in our lives, attracting things which share a similar vibration and energy to us. With that understanding, your main goal is to focus on feeling good! Get into the energy of who you want to be and how it FEELS to live the life you're co-creating. The "how" and "what it looks like", that bit isn't your job. Your job is knowing how it feels and then allowing yourself to FEEL IT right now!

3. It's already done.

    I'm a recovering controller, worrier, and over-analyzer, so this "surrender" step can sometimes trip me up. Letting go isn't easy and takes practice (the Universe knows I've had to learn the hard way). However, when I fully surrender and know that it's done, true magic always follows. It never fails. Give it up and turn over your darn calendar. It'll happen when it happens. The thing to remember is that you must surrender and TRUST that it WILL happen. Trust that it is coming your way, even if it's not according to your "timeline" or if it doesn't look like you imagined. The Universe has a better plan anyways...and guess what? It knows all about this little thing called divine timing.

Let it go and know that it's already done.

We're all in the process of becoming the truest versions of ourselves. This is a journey. Each day you're making decisions to show up as her, to take action, to be vulnerable and scared, to get uncomfortable, and to grow. It's an ongoing process of self-development and expansion. It gets messy, with many exciting and stomach-churning twists and turns, but there's a simple secret weapon to it all. It's one I learned a little later in life, but do you want in on it?

It is: ENJOY THIS PROCESS!

Huh? I hear your thoughts: "This is supposed to be fun?"

Heck yes, it's fun! Be excited about this journey, so that nothing can slow you down! Embrace each moment, be present, and find the beauty and joy exactly where you are…and within everything.

"Now! Go!

Stake your claim! Hold out your hands. Move, get ready, give thanks. Imagine, and let go.

Act, and have faith. Persist.
Do what you can, when you can, all you can.
Because never again, not in a million years, over ten thousand lifetimes, will you ever be as close as you are today."
The Universe (TUT.Com)

ABOUT LIZ REDDICK

A Canadian speaker, author, and mindset coach, Liz is dedicated to helping women (especially mothers) reconnect with their purpose and joy. Her work is focused on supporting and guiding women as they step into their power and realize their full potential. It was after having children herself that Liz discovered her real passion for coaching mothers, aiding and guiding them as they discover their dreams, desires, ambitions, and inner strength.

In addition to her coaching career, Liz also runs a successful marketing and consulting business. She has channeled her 16 years of experience in the fields of communication and marketing into providing services for female entrepreneurs who also have a passion for serving others and creating positive change.

Liz is a master of moving mountains, and the first person to roll up their sleeves and help you to move your own. Her ability to visualize where she wants to go, and then get there, is second to none. So much of the life she lives and enjoys today is because of this tenacious attitude and the desire to be the best version of herself that she can be.

Connect with Liz:

E-mail: Liz@lizreddick.com

Instagram: https://www.instagram.com/liz.reddick/

Facebook: https://www.facebook.com/simplylizreddick

Website: https://lizreddick.com/

No Magic Glitter is Needed to Have it All... Just a Little SPARKLE!

Kelly Withers

So, WE ALL KNOW THAT MOM. YOU KNOW, THE ONE THAT has the perfect hair and nails, perfect outfit, perfect career, perfect body and every time you see her has a smile on her face while saying *"Good Morning"* to everyone in the most positive way. All this while your hair is in a bun, in your yoga pants for the third day hoping these are not the see through ones, have no idea if you remembered to brush your teeth or put deodorant on, feel like you have not slept in a week and have no idea how you will catch up at work because you are so behind. So, you think to yourself..."*what the **** Am I doing wrong?*"

The answer is *NOTHING!*

You just need a little bit of a plan to find your inner sparkle, and I am here to help you shine!

I have days where I am both of those moms! Some days I wake up at four a.m., get my run in, shower, have my hair and makeup on before the family is up and make a healthy breakfast from scratch for everyone. That whole time knowing I am going to crush the day and do it in a positive way saying *"hello"* to everyone I see. Then, somehow, I wake up the next day at seven a.m., throw on a pair of yoga pants I found on the floor hoping no one notices the stain, forgot I was supposed to help my kindergartener do his homework the night before as I am shoving Cheetos in his book bag for lunch and pray I do not get a speeding ticket on the way to work as my five year old is eating potato chips for breakfast. However, at the end of both days, both nights end up the same... snuggling on the couch with my family and enjoying a nice glass or two of wine. I know I am just doing the best I can and accepting my highs and lows. I have learned to embrace and celebrate each and every day.

I can honestly tell you I did not get to this place of having everything I wanted overnight. Just like everyone else, I have stumbled, I have failed, I have cried, I have had days where I just wanted to give up, but I always focused on knowing what I wanted for the big picture and just kept a positive attitude despite any obstacles.

So where am I today and why should you listen to me? I am an IVF mom - after seven years and more infertility treatments than anyone should ever have to endure - to an amazing five-year-old miracle Kade, wife to my husband Kyle who is my partner in crime and biggest support system, former national NPC bikini competitor, a successful career woman at the director level and independent business owner since 2007. I worked my booty off for every single one of these accomplishments and I continue to work my booty off every day to maintain these accomplishments. All of these situations came with their own unique set of obstacles and challenges, but I never gave up and despite lots of let downs and disappointments. I always picked myself back up and kept going. I always had and still have the inner determination to be the best I can and go after my dreams. I am fully confident that you can too, if you just choose to have that positive attitude, put one shoe in front of the other to keep going and not look back. Or, if you are like me, those shoes are actually some bright pink heels!

We have all been in a place where our lives are so chaotic that all you want to do is just lay on the couch, fall asleep and hope some magic fairy godmother fixes it by the time you wake up.

Truth is…. *YOU are that fairy godmother!*

The truth is *NO ONE is perfect!*

I know, crazy right? The big secret is finally out after all these years.

The truth is, no one else, other than you, can make this change.

So that perfect mom doesn't have the perfect life behind closed doors. No one does! However, what we are all capable of, is the perfect life for ourselves and realizing we have the inner power to achieve anything we set our minds to. What that looks like is different for everyone and you have to be willing to sometimes take a step back before you take a step forward.

First of all, you are doing amazing! Recognize that being a female in itself comes with challenges and sometimes we are constantly fighting an upward battle. It is okay to fail. It is okay if you forgot to pack your kid's lunch for school one day. They will still eat. It is okay if you let the dishes sit in the sink and they start to pile up. It is okay if you wear your hair in a bun to work two days in a row - just throw on some cute earrings so that everyone notices those super cute earrings and not the messy five-day bun. It is okay if you cannot make it to the gym before work, because you hit the snooze button for that extra thirty minutes knowing your body needs that extra rest: do some booty squeezes while you are driving to work or sitting at your desk. Recognizing yourself, learning to give yourself some credit, and realizing your potential is key to beginning your journey to finding your inner sparkle and getting ready to be a glow getter!

Second, it is time to form a game plan! Everything starts with a plan; whether it's an architect building a house, a new business getting started or mapping out the details of your Disney vacation. Building a timeline and putting together an overall plan with mile markers along the way is how you will start to get things moving in the right direction. I like to say, *"Life is not a track meet… it is a marathon."* I think that line actually came from a 90's rap song, but the meaning behind that line is so true! Besides, everyone can use a little music for motivation! In order to cross that finish line, you need to pass every mile marker. The same philosophy applies in life. Figure out what your long-term plan is, and then plan out all the steps that are needed along the way to get to that finish line. Celebrate every goal you hit! No goal is too small. Even if that goal is just taking a shower, washing your hair and doing thirty squats while you brush your teeth. Celebrate it! It is all about the baby steps and giving yourself some credit! Then, even if you have to "cheers" to yourself, heck yeah, pour that glass of Prosecco and celebrate!

Thirdly, invest in yourself. Find something you enjoy to do and allow yourself the time to fully invest yourself. For me, it is working out. I love to hit the gym, pop in my air pods and just focus on some fun motivational music that gets me pumped. Maybe for you, it is yoga. Maybe it is reading a book. Maybe it is meditation. Maybe it is going to the spa once a week. I mean we would all definitely like to add that one to our list! My point is just to find something where you can let it all go, so you can gather your thoughts and just focus on yourself. Investing in yourself and your own mental, emotional and physical well-being are crucial in personal success.

Fourthly, it is okay to tell people NO. If you are anything like me, you are a people pleaser and you hate the thought of letting people down. Your time is precious and you need to treat it that way. If you cannot pick up a friend's kids, say no. If you would rather go home and spend time with your family than going to happy hour with your work colleagues, it is okay to say no. Your true family and friends, that love and respect you, will understand setting boundaries. Once you say no, commit to it! Don't spend the next few hours dwelling on the fact that you said no. Embrace your strength and celebrate your willpower.

Finally, write things down. Keep a journal so you are holding yourself responsible. I write down my short- and long-term goals, the food I eat, my workouts, and my thoughts. I also try to commit to daily motivational quotes. The power of positive thoughts are so important for manifesting. I actually use one of my five-year old's bath crayons and often write my goals or quotes in the shower. Hey, you gotta do what you can do, right? Accountability is so important, because without holding yourself accountable...no one else is going to. When you write things down and read them, you can truly start to assess if you are progressing forward or if you are just making excuses.

Now that we have a road map in place, it is time to implement it. Nothing will happen if you do not commit to making a change. I repeat, *nothing will happen if you do not commit to a change.* This can actually be the hardest step of the journey; however, it is one of the most important steps. Just like Rome was not built in a day, you will not change your life in a day. This commitment to change is extremely powerful. It has potential to change your life and get it headed in the direction you want to go. It is like when you are ready to start that diet, you hired a personal trainer, bought all the right foods and are ready to go, or are you? It is one thing to have the game plan, but it is a whole different thing to cross that start line. It is time to run, walk or crawl across that start line and just worry about you. Do not worry about the competition. YOU are your only competition and whatever your pace is...that is your pace. So, strap on those stilettos and put on your favorite shade of lip gloss because it is about to rain and sparkle glitter everywhere!

My challenge to you is to just try the things I listed and truly commit to them. Surround yourself with positive people and weed out the negative people or things in your life that are bringing you down. Negativity is draining and consumes way more of your time and energy when you can be devoting that energy towards positivity.

The reason why my favorite word is SPARKLE, is because it represents a glistening, shimmering, shining and sense of positivity.

So, are you going to find your inner SPARKLE?

Just imagine having a sparkle to your step anytime you go anywhere or walk into a room. That inner sparkle will give you the confidence to smile every single day. On good days, bad days and the days where you end up somewhere in between.

It is time to find that outfit that makes you feel amazing, grab your computer or journal and start your journey to being that strong female capable of crushing all of your goals!

#SPARKLEANDSTEEL

ABOUT KELLY WITHERS

Kelly Withers is a busy mom that knows how to have it all with a smile on her face and a little bit of pink glitter and sparkle. She has a never give up attitude and tenacity to complete any task given to her. She balances a full-time career as a Regional Director for a medical device company, has a booming personal training business and is an IVF warrior with a five-year-old and a second IVF baby coming early 2021.

She knows that momming isn't easy and daily struggles are a part of life and it is all about finding the magic key to figure out a way that when your head hits the pillow at night you crash with a smile on your face knowing you did the best you could!

Her focus is on helping women gain that confidence to find a way to overcome obstacles and find a balance in their life and do it all with a smile. Find your inner sparkle with Kelly and uncover how to turn that stressful day around!

@Kelly.aesthetics.fitness on Instagram

www.sparkleandsteel.com

Awaken Your Inner Fire

Laura Beth Mathews

IN 2013 I WAS DIAGNOSED WITH PCOS (POLYCYSTIC ovarian syndrome), and I was told I most likely would never conceive. Over the next few years, I went through so much testing. The last one was in December of 2015. I had a hysterosalpingogram, which is when they inject dye through your cervix to see if your tubes are blocked. My doctor said if I have a blocked fallopian tube, sometimes the dye will open them up. After an hour of agony (I would never do this again without a Valium!), the radiologist said my right tube was blocked. *Sigh* My doctor called me and said that even if it was unblocked, we might not be able to conceive for at least a year. Well, God had a different plan! Three months later, I was pregnant.

March 18, 2016. I was supposed to get my menstrual cycle this week. I normally spot at least three days before and start getting cramps. I felt a little cramping a few days before, and I asked my friend for an ibuprofen. She looked at me and asked, "Are you pregnant?" I said,

"No! Why the hell would I be pregnant?" Fast forward to the 18th, and I was running around work like usual. At lunch, I finally was able to relax and realized I had no cramping whatsoever. I knew something was going on, because this is not like me to have no cramps.

My gut nudged me to take a pregnancy test.

I couldn't wait to get home from work to pee on a stick, but I had so much anxiety. Could I really be pregnant? I took one out of the box and took it.

Wait... is this a faint line?

Oh my GOD!! I think it is! I examined it for twenty minutes! I even took a picture and sent it to a few friends. They confirmed that it indeed looked like a faint line.

This can't be possible!

The next day, mainly to validate it for myself, I went to Target and got the Clearblue Digital. I couldn't make a mistake in reading one that literally said pregnant or not pregnant, right?

I took the test and it came back positive 1-2 weeks!!

Oh my GOD! I'm PREGNANT! Son of a gun, my friend was right!

I was so excited!

I went to my doctor for blood work to have a more official result and it too was positive. Because of my past health issues, my OB wanted to monitor me closely. I had my first ultrasound at five and a half weeks and for the first time, I saw my baby's heartbeat. It became more real for me. There is nothing in this world that can compare to the love that I felt for this tiny little life in me.

Then it happened. I started spotting. I went for more blood work at my doctor's, and was assured that everything was fine. I sighed a huge breath of relief, but the anxious spot in my stomach stayed.

Then at seven and half weeks, I had another bleeding episode, but this one was major. I was so scared! I went for an emergency ultrasound and was once again assured the baby was fine. However, I still had a little bleeding and at that point, my doctor wanted to be safe rather than sorry with how we proceeded. My doctor ordered me on bedrest and to have a follow up ultrasound the following week to keep everything in check.

I followed the orders of bedrest strictly. The following week my fiancé and I went for the ultrasound. When I asked if we were going to get to see the baby this time, she stayed quiet. I immediately felt a knot in my gut. I knew this was bad news. We were then taken to the exam room. My doctor came in and uttered the words no expecting parent wants to hear, "There is no heartbeat."

In just a matter of seconds, our world was shattered into a million broken pieces. I felt as if I could not breathe. Surely, this was a nightmare and I would wake up.

The next year of my life would be a rollercoaster of emotions. I was angry with myself. I was angry with God. I felt guilty that I didn't ask for more bloodwork. Did I eat the wrong foods? Did that morning coffee do this? All of the self-guilt I laid onto myself was thick and suffocating. I felt guilty that I had caused my baby to die. I was embarrassed that I could not keep a pregnancy. A full range of emotions took over.

The emotions flooded me. So many emotions came over me that eventually it got to a point where they were just too much. I wanted to end it all! I couldn't take it anymore. I needed a way out. That moment of hopelessness, that wanting to just end it all...it brought me back to when I was thirteen years old. I was in a place that I *never* wanted to go back to. I knew I didn't want to be there again. At that point, I prayed and begged for The Universe to show me what to do. Immediately, The Universe answered and I was then guided to enroll into The Institute of Integrative Nutrition. I thought, "Okay, well at least I can learn how to heal my body through food." I listened to The Universe.

Then, I found Gabby Bernstein. I kept seeing her name on my suggested people to follow on Instagram.

Every time I saw her name, I felt a nudge to follow her. One day, I finally clicked the follow button. How thankful and glad I am that I did. She helped open up new doors of healing and light into my life that I did not know about up until this point. This is how I learned about meditation, spirit guides, and trusting God and The Universe. I immersed myself in learning from her. I read all her books. I took all her workshops. I learned anything I could from her. I also took her Spirit Junkie Masterclass in 2019, which was so much more valuable than I expected.

This new path in spirituality eventually led me to yoga! Yoga changed my life. I am starting my yoga teacher training and will be certified in June 2021. I am so excited, because I have been wanting to get my teacher training since 2017! Yoga has been such a vital part of my healing. It has revealed hidden trauma that I didn't even know was there. It helped me to open up, clear space, and create more room for what I desired in my life. After leaning into yoga and using it to heal in so many ways. Once again, I found myself thinking, "Ok, now what?" The Universe heard me and once again delivered to me the next step of my journey.

I kept listening to my intuition and it guided me to Reiki and Kundalini yoga. I didn't even know what these were until two years ago. I had a friend who was a Reiki Master and I had a session with her. Wow, that was such a healing session! I saw colors and at one point I saw white glowing hands pulling black gunk out of my throat. I asked her what the black gunk was and she said that my throat chakra was extremely blocked. Wow! I was inspired and wanted to learn more. This is when I was introduced to Holy Fire® Reiki through another great friend of mine. This guided me to take the first two levels and then move on to master training. This, coupled with Kundalini yoga, has brought up and healed so much past life and childhood trauma.

I had no idea just how many memories and emotions I had repressed over the years. I blamed my fiancé for being controlling (which was not the case at all!) and finally after the childhood trauma came to the surface, I realized he was just a mirror of what I needed to heal inside me. This doesn't have to be romantic relationships either; every relationship we encounter is a mirror and a trigger. You may be the mirror and trigger for the other person. I love shadow work and peeling back the layers of finding my authentic self. Is it easy? Absolutely not. There were many times that I was bawling on the floor releasing and healing whatever needed to come up to the surface, but it is worth the tears. What you get is a life of abundance, happiness, and true joy.

Although, shadow work and healing is never done. As you ascend higher, the lessons will still be there. They will be different, but still there. Friends that are not of the highest good for your life will start falling away. That job you can't stand will go. The toxic relationship that you didn't know how to leave will go. You will start questioning your very existence. Then, everything will come together and it will be 1000% better than you've ever dreamed of.

They say hindsight is 20/20, and I guess that's true. After years of healing and working on myself, I finally saw the silver lining of the miscarriage. Writing this was also another healing journey. As I wrote this, I was hysterically crying. Even though I healed from the miscarriage, I didn't realize how much pain I had buried. This was truly a blessing to be able to share my story with you. The healing that I have gone through is amazing. I am finally at peace with every aspect of my life! My friendships are more meaningful, and I have the best friendship with the love of my life (thanks, babe, for loving me even at my worst!) Ladies, a word of advice: if you have someone who sticks by you and loves you at the lowest point in your life, they are a keeper!!

Today, I find myself working with women who are wanting more out of life. Who are wondering what their purpose in the world is. Who need the support and help to heal. Who are ready to spread their wings and put in the work. This journey of healing is why I feel so called to help and guide women who are in that same place that I was. I want them to experience the peace and healing

I felt. To be able to see things from a new perspective. To be able to rid themselves of the negative thoughts and patterns. To find their true purpose. To truly LOVE themselves. To help raise the vibration of Mother Gaia, and to heal future generations.

Believe me, YOU can be at peace.

YOU can heal.

YOU can be free.

All you need are the tools, a mentor, and the willingness to do so. That's why I created my 90-day one-on-one signature program called Awaken Your Inner Fire. We dive very deep into your energy meridians, cellular repair, chakras, and organs. We will also heal relationships, will dive into shadow work, heal any sexual and/or physical abuse, past life issues and trauma, heal any karma that is left for you, and heal any addictions. There are weekly 90-minute calls that are split into a half an hour for a reiki session and the other hour will be for coaching. Also, there are weekly crystal sound bowl meditations that are tailored to meet your needs for that week, Kundalini Kriyas, journal prompts, monthly oracle card readings, and much more.

We are much more powerful when we are healed, happy, and abundant. When we are of service to others, it helps raise the vibration and consciousness of the planet. I am so ready for the next upgrade in my life. Yes, 2020 was a complete mess, but so much has come together. Are you ready to live the life you deserve? Let's get it done in 2021!!!

ABOUT LAURA BETH MATHEWS

Laura Beth Mathews is a Spiritual Coach and Teacher, Holy Fire® lll Karuna Reiki Master Teacher, Atlantean Quantum Healer, Motivational Speaker, Yogi, Meditation Teacher, Spirit Junkie Masterclass Level 1 Alumni, and Crystal lover. She guides women to discover their purpose and to finally put themselves first through energy healing and spiritual coaching.

Her methodology is a blend of energetic healing through Kundalini Yoga, Reiki, Crystal Sound Bowl Meditations, and busting through energetic blocks through Atlantean Quantum Healing and EFT (Emotional Freedom Technique aka tapping). She has perfected these energy modalities, as these are the tools that helped heal her during her spiritual awakening. Through this deep energetic work, her clients have bust through the energetic blocks that have held them back, and have healed their limiting beliefs and childhood traumas to become the Goddesses that they have always been and to live the lives that they deserve.

From a young age, she felt connected to spirit, nature, and had a deep inner knowing that she was on this earth to make a difference. As she got older, like many of us, that feeling dimmed until she was awakened in April of 2016 when she had a missed miscarriage.

At that low point, she found the Institute for Integrative Nutrition, enrolled, and in time became an Integrative Nutrition Health Coach.

She has transformed her life in ways that she NEVER thought she would. She found her spiritual practice by learning from the likes of Gabby Bernstein, and learned how to meditate. She also brought yoga into her life and now she lives her life in love, light, and abundance!

It was a long road to get here, but she has arrived! Of course, there are moments of ups and downs (that's what being human IS), but with the tools she has found she is able to return to love very quickly.

With Laura as your coach and healer, she will teach you what she has learned and will guide you through your rock bottom to live the life you deserve.

Website:
laurabethmathews.com

Instagram:
https://www.instagram.com/iamlaurabethmathews/

Twitter:
https://twitter.com/lauramathews86

Facebook:
https://www.facebook.com/LauraBethMathews

Book a session:
https://laurabethmathewsschedule.as.me/

Speak Life Unapologetically

Melysa Aldiano

WHO WOULD HAVE THOUGHT THAT A MILESTONE birthday of me turning forty years old would have been in global pandemic crisis? 2020 has brought humanity immense pain, sorrow, natural disaster, and many of us are still grieving for the loss of loved ones, too. We lost people that are dear to our heart. Opinions are oscillating on both sides. Many have said, "I hope this pandemic will teach the mankind the lessons of their lives." or "People will finally realize what's matters most." and the list goes on.

However, in my situation, 2020 has brought me tremendous gifts! God given gifts that He activates in me, I believe, because the world needs another soul to spread and share the words of wisdom, best experiences, and lessons in life that I was taught and had learned.

There are numerous souls who are in desperate need to know who you are and what you are...

Looking back from what I've gone through, including my past pains and the struggles and adversities I had to face starting from my childhood up until I became a woman, one quote summarizes it all:

"I swam a lot of rivers."

I had a fairly normal childhood. I was raised carrying the faith to God that my mother had taught me. Simultaneously, I was witnessing the abusive drinking, multiple adulteries, and abandonment from my father that enormously impacted my entire well-being.

I grew up seeing my father seeking comfort in other places and people rather than his own family. There are few memories I have of him that I treasure: him teaching me to ride a bicycle and his love for music. My father's aggressions at home were hard to watch as a small girl. I felt the need to protect my mother from his anger that stemmed from alcohol, partying, abuse, and adultery. This caused my mother to work extra hard to have our needs provided and so we had quality schooling. In spite of everything she experienced with my father, she showed us love and kept our faith in God.

When I turned eighteen, I had to stand on my own. I decided to live abroad, and my father betrayed me once again upon my refusal to marry a wealthy man. He called me "ungrateful" and "selfish." These words caused me to push forward, stand up, and use my voice. All that I endured created a resilience and determination in me to keep moving forward.

Yet, I felt as if I was in a battle...a battle of my own emotion, perhaps? However, fate had a distinct plan for me, and I had no clue.

Years of paving the road of opportunities were filled with ups and downs in building episodes in each chapter in my life. I was simply becoming the author of my story.

I married and divorced the father of my first child, a beautiful son. I now have a great friendship with my first husband. In my early thirties, I met a dance partner on a dance floor, who later became the father of my beautiful daughter and my life partner as well.

Although I was fortunate to have attracted the right partner, here I was with my heart shattered, mind disoriented, and feeling completely lost! Despite all the blessings and abundance, this is how I felt. I did not understand why.

In full transparency, I gained the courage to speak with my partner. I told him three things:

"Please set me free. I need space to set all things together."

"I am seeking conclusive answers in my life; I have no clue what they are."

"Perhaps I'm looking for myself, as I feel completely lost, despite everything I am fortunate to have."

At first, he thought I was leaving, but I wasn't. I later explained to him how I truly felt, my deepest notions I couldn't voice at the time. I was seeking answers, answers to what more life had to offer me or a purpose for me waiting to be defined. I knew life had an unwavering plan for me, I just needed to dig in deep and chase after it. There was a huge desire of something very unknown, scary, and daunting. Then, my journey began…

In the course of my innovative journey, through years of infinite incidents of life, I had to face countless encounters that have landed me in different spaces. I am beyond grateful.

2020 is the year of my transformation. I highly believe in synchronicity and that nothing is coincidence. We put in our time and energy with every action we commit to. When 2020 began, I intentionally chose the people to surround myself with online and offline. To be able to reach a certain level of people, I had to ensure that I was ready to let go of the things that do not serve me. This included family, friends, acquaintances, and co-workers. This is crucial for your growth and definitely your success! It may sound egocentric or self-centered, but setting boundaries is imperative and I highly recommend it. First, candidly acknowledge the things in your daily life that don't work for your personal growth. Secondly, be aware of and acknowledge the people in your environment.

I asked myself these questions:

"What are my deepest pains and adversities that became the catalysts of who I am today and who I am evolving into?"

"What was the greatest challenge I faced in my past?"

"What was the first step I took in overcoming my obstacles… and how did I overcome them?"

These were the first three significant questions I asked myself. Then, I started digging deep on what I should do. What are some alterations in my life that are attainable for me? There was only one thing I could think of:

Acknowledging my fears and my obstacles!

I started being utterly honest with myself and in full transparency to others to comprehend those obstacles that were hindering my personal growth. In December 2019, I had worked for a company for more than ten years. I felt like I was dying inside, plus I felt depressed and suppressed for years. I couldn't let that continue to happen because of my children. They needed a mother who cared for them, a mother who brought them joy and love. I needed to pull myself together in order to understand what my biggest "why" was: my children. Not long after questioning myself, I gained the courage to leave that corporate job. I acted and negotiated it to my advantage, without leaving an unnecessary conception of pessimism. I never had a second of regret.

Then, I start investing in my personal growth. I truly believe that you don't meet people by accident. Every person you meet has a divine purpose. There are some people who are in your life for season and are merely passing by. They are there to either love you, hurt you, or teach you. Then, there are lifetime people that will build a strong fundamental basis of your growth and successes. Those relationships may turn from collaborations into significant friendships. I started collaborating with high-level, impactful people who all helped me to work on myself. Once again, I am beyond blessed and fortunate to have encountered these kinds of people; this only manifested that I am here for a greater purpose that I wasn't fully aware of just yet…

Healing has no end. In the beginning of my process, I wrote several letters to people, including a few to myself. I wrote a letter confronting that hurt little girl "Melysa" in which I said to her:

*"I'm sorry for not knowing better, and for being innocent.
I'm sorry you had to undergo all that hurts and rejection at a very
young age."*

*"I'm sorry that I wasn't there for you to tell you that all the
pains you have gone through weren't for nothing."*

*"All the hurdles, abandonment, and exclusion were the best
life lessons and best life experiences you could ever have, that I
could ever have…"*

I had to fully let go of all the pains and brokenness.
I had to face my unhealed, buried pains and work on
them. I had to overcome all the hurdles and unspoken
words that had been concealed for decades. I cried over
and over again, confronting myself and acknowledging
those pains. I would think of all those memories that
had been a huge burden to me. I would cry out from rage
and anger, feeling powerless. Little did I know that there
was a remedy. Even though you cannot undo things that
have already occurred, you can learn how to deal with
it. You can defy the odds and move on with your life. I
wasn't aware of any of this. I thought that I could simply
move on without having to talk about it or put the past
in the past. I didn't realize there were huge consequences
attached to this behavior, but I would discover that later.

In the course of all this, I have learned to fully ground
myself and operate from within. To awaken and unleash
the desire that lies beneath.

I have also come to realize that you do not fix a broken heart. Instead, you heal it. You transform your pain into a positive energy to derive a cognitive outcome. You convert your deepest pain into your divine aligned purpose. But in order to get there you have to be ready to resist, to defy all the inconveniences and biases. The so-called ego "losing face" is one of the biggest reasons why people don't dare to acknowledge and admit their most unspoken words.

While this part of my journey is continuously emerging, I have learned to forgive the people who have caused me pain in the past, mostly my father. I have asked for forgiveness from my mother. Perhaps the most difficult of all, I have learned to forgive myself. I've learned that it's okay to not feel okay all the time, and it's okay if things don't go the way I want them to. It's fine to fall down as long as you rise up again even stronger.

I asked for forgiveness from God. I asked God to forgive me for questioning Him throughout the years and for not abiding His words of wisdom and learnings. I asked God to guide me on this walk of life I am stepping into. We will never succeed acting solo, only through His guidance and help can we succeed. He will put the right people on our path. I have learned to surrender all my worries and queries that were far beyond my comprehension. I have learned to filter the people in my environment, especially people that were only there occasionally. It's important to empty spaces and make some room for the right people in your life: the people that will uplift you, make you a better person, and who will have your back in times of uncertainties.

We can't forget that some people in our lives will use us until our heart shatters! Fear not, because God will use them to take us higher! It is astonishing and simply phenomenal how significantly your life can change when you stop allowing what doesn't serve you.

These were part of the conclusive occurrences that were taking place at the beginning of 2020. I can only be grateful for them.

A global pandemic was in the midst of my healing process, and in those countless sleepless nights, I am beyond grateful to meet my true self. I have found my divine inner peace that I was seeking for years. I've never felt so deeply liberated before. It's as if this was the time for me to truly understand why things happened the way they did in my life, as if this is the right moment for me to evolve. I have not only found my inner peace, but my faith towards God. I now cannot disregard His significant divine works that keep showing up in my life.

While this apparent life-changing was taking place, I obtained the courage to put a short story of my life journey that had all started when I was just eight years old on one of my social media platforms. This was one of my homework assignments from a coaching session of why I became the person I used to be and why I worked on becoming a better version of my previous self.

My online friends started sending me private messages of their profound feedback about the short story I had posted.

They said:

"How brave of you to reveal your story to the world!"

"You are so courageous to have overcome all those pains and adversities, especially coming from your own father!"

"How fearless you are to speak up for yourself!"

In reality, I was still confronting that little hurt girl; it wasn't always sunshine and roses for me! However, the most ironic feedback I received on that day was a friend asking me,

"Are you considering to be a writer or an author? "

"You will inspire many souls of your story. ."

"You will be able to help them to overcome their own fears."

"You will inspire others to find their purpose."

Shortly afterwards, my network started to broaden. As I always believe that we don't meet people by accident, an online friend of mine introduced me to a truly beautiful soul who was working on a book project. I started communicating with her and immediately felt this aligned connection with her. That connection led me to write and contribute a chapter in the book series. Once again, I acted, did things that were far beyond my comprehension, and I definitely surpassed my own expectations! I hadn't thought in the immediate future I would be ready to reveal and share my story to the world! This alone sounded quite challenging and petrifying to me, until I started writing it. I would get emotional from time to time, remembering the love infused with pain.

Months after working on my first co-authored book chapter, I became more self-confident and candidly at peace. I acted and spoke from my heart intentionally. I was aware of what I spoke of and acted with, and it lined up with my actions and words.

The time came that we were about to launch our book, in the time of uncertainty. One of my biggest dreams became my reality: not only did the book reach the number one best seller list on Amazon, it reached the international best seller list! This meant that I, who also contributed on the book series, became an international best-selling author! I could only imagine this in my dreams.

People started to connect with me more often, especially people coming from high-level spaces and different continents. Some of them simply approached and asked to collaborate with me. In addition to that, people have asked me locally to speak at their events! I said, "Yes!" Due to Covid-19 measurements and restricted travel policy, I also received more invitations to speak on online platforms and to share my story. This was not merely to inspire, but rather to aspire and motivate people and their purpose.

A dear friend of mine told me to not feel overwhelmed, as this was just the beginning of my divine aligned purpose that God had put me into. These were the long-awaited answers to the questions I had asked years ago. I truly believe that everyone of us has a greater cause in this beautiful yet wicked world. Each of us is solely trying their best to make a difference and leave a meaningful, significant legacy to the next generations.

All that I had done was far beyond my comprehension, but this isn't about me! It's about serving others. I share my story to the world not merely to narrate what I've gone through in the past, but rather to show the humanity that the pains I've experienced and occurred to me have shaped me into who I am today. It all became the catalyst of who I've transformed into today, and it is still evolving; I am still evolving.

Sharing my wisdom...and always being a student of life.

Aiming higher is human behavior! Craving for adventures and explorations! Being hungry to learn and seeking answers for more in life! I am one of those people too, and there is nothing wrong with that. As long as we walk on our path in humility, humbleness, showing immense gratitude always, and live a life with integrity in tandem with your actions and words.

It never was about me or you. It is all about serving others and how we can help serve humanity. It's about creating great leaders in our children! This is making a difference and leaving a significant legacy.

I won't forget where I came from, but I will inevitably focus on the paved road of opportunities on which I stand.

I dared to stand up! I have learned to speak up!

I was courageous to transform my life into becoming a healed servant leader.

I celebrate and speak life unapologetically.

I will always say this: put God as the center of your life. Because He is capable of all the impossible! We are nothing without our faith towards Him.

Hebrew 4:16 says, *"Let us then approach God's throne*

of grace with confidence, so that we may receive mercy and find grace to help us in our time of need."

Powerful and true.

Surrender all your worries. No matter how confused you are and uncomfortable it might seem to you, the Biblical phrase of Matthew 7:7-8 says, *"Ask, and it will be given to you; seek, and you will find; knock, and it will be opened to you. For everyone who asks receives, and the one who seeks finds, and to the one who knocks, it will be opened."*

As whatever you speak of, comes to life…

ABOUT MELYSA ALDIANO

Melysa Aldiano was born and raised in Laguna, Philippines. She attended The State Polytechnic University in Santa Cruz, Laguna where she received a Bachelor of Science in Electronics Engineering. She was the youngest of the crowd, but one of the top performers in her major.

During the summer of 1998, Melysa decided to move to Austria. She lived there for almost a decade and she laid another foundation of her life. In 2006, she moved to Belgium where she now lives a joyful and harmonious life with her two beautiful children, Daniel and Aurora-Victoria, and life partner Marc.

Melysa is a student of life. She loves learning languages, reading, and mindfulness. Her passion in her spare time is dance and music. She is an avid Latin dancer, adventurer, outside person, and free spirit. She loves fashion and she's a shoe addict.

Her diverse creative talents have landed her into different platforms in her career, like living abroad, in which she found her second home. After decades of seeking her divine aligned purpose, in 2019 she began investing in herself. She put an end to working in the corporate world and finally decided to take the steer of her career. Melysa found herself investing in personal development and one-on-one mentorship; it's the best investment, she says!

Melysa is an influencer, a thought leader, an entrepreneur, an International Best-selling author, and a speaker.

She created a community called the JOY UNFILTERED Movement, which is a community where thrivers, game-changers, and doers can come together to create a global positive ripple effect. She wants to lead a movement that celebrates authenticity, positivity, and fulfillment; a movement that celebrates and radiates life!

Melysa focuses on helping women, through "What Is A True Woman of Influence?" "How to Live Unapologetically" and "How to Live A Life in Purpose"; these are the foundations and pillars of the JOY UNFILTERED Movement.

Melysa believes that a great future doesn't require a great past. Genuine happiness starts of being at peace with yourself and putting God in the center of your life, always.

Social Media Handles and Contact:

Facebook: Melysa Aldiano

Facebook Page: JOY Unfiltered Movement

https://www.facebook.com/joyunfilteredmovement/

Instagram: @ joy_unfiltered

E-mail: aldianomelysa@gmail.com

Melysa Aldiano - Consulting & Coaching

Sober Eyes

Tabitha Seefeldt

I WILL NEVER BE ABLE TO FEEL SAFE AGAIN. "THAT" IS WHAT I told myself after that traumatic day. What he did to me was so much more than abuse, he had me all messed up in my head now, too. The only way I could handle being around people was if I was drunk, my anxiety was so bad that I didn't know how to be around anyone unless I had a few drinks in me. No one knew that I was drinking as much as I was. I started just having a few drinks every now and then. Before I knew it, I was drinking every weekend just to get drunk. *What was happening to me?* *Why was I doing this? Why did I feel like I needed to drink every weekend? Why did I feel like I needed to prove something when I went out?* I felt like that was the only way to hide my pain on the inside. I thought this was the only way to feel accepted. I felt if I was the fun girl I would be the one other people would want to hang around with. My entire life I spent trying to fit into someone else's mold and the drinking was just another turn down that same path, but this time I was spiraling downward way too quickly.

I'll never forget one night I was bartending in one of the small towns back home and a bunch of the locals came in. They asked to play bar dice and so I did. I ended up losing a lot and would have to take shots for losing. I did not know how to say NO to them back then, as I was still living in fear of saying NO to men. I got so damn drunk that I don't remember anything from the rest of the night. I had apparently danced on the bar, sprayed everyone with the hose and gave away free drinks. That night they needed to not only call me a ride home, but they also needed to call my boss in to close the bar at bar close. I was so embarrassed the next day that I didn't want to go back there. Looking back now, not only do I realize how foolish it was, but also how lucky I was that they actually made sure nothing happened to me, that I didn't attempt to drive home, or even worse, that someone could've tried to take advantage of me.

One night, as I was sitting out on the deck drinking with my aunt and I kept asking myself is this really the life that I want? Do I really want to look forward to the weekends just to drink and get drunk for the rest of my life? I was feeling so lost, alone, afraid and scared. I had moved away from home after my abusive relationship. I feared for my life daily until he was locked up. I didn't want to be in the same town as him. He had posted bail and was awaiting the jury trial to convict him, so I had left town. One day, I had a new message on my Myspace (yes, you read that correctly) account from a good friend of mine. He mentioned my friend thinks you're hot and wants to meet you. I totally laughed it off and told him that he was crazy. He sent another message and was asking me to come back to town for one weekend just to meet this guy. He knew what I had gone through, so my friend was well aware that I was not really looking for any type of relationship at that time. I finally caved in. I agreed to drive back up there to meet this guy and see what that fuss was about. That guy I met is now my husband Brad, we celebrated ten years of marriage this year.

The night I agreed to meet this guy I got drunk once again. As the night went on, I was out with a bunch of friends and we swear to this day that someone slipped something in all of our drinks. It was definitely a night none of us will ever forget. When this guy I was supposed to meet finally showed up, I took one look at him and was like: Nope, not happening. He's a total player. He had these girls hanging all over him and I wanted nothing to do with that or his arrogant vibe. Brad and I ended up exchanging numbers that night, and I told him that when he was ready to stop being a player then he should give me a call. He went about his night and was buying drinks and shots for everyone. The thought of a partying guy was starting to attract me to him more, but I had a track record for liking the bad boys my entire dating season.

The next day, we ended up texting each other and almost every day thereafter for over two weeks before I finally agreed to one date with him. When the night of our first date happened, you guessed it, we had drinks. Who would go on a date sober? Things went really well, surprisingly. We continued to text and call one another for the next three weeks. I decided to move up to his town (crazy I know, but I just had a feeling this could be it) and that's when the shift started to happen. I moved up and we started going out every single weekend. We would just get wasted or at least I know I did many times. We would stay out until the bar closed and even have a few drinks once we got back to his house afterwards. I started getting sick almost every single time and you know what, this guy took care of me. He held my hair as I puked my brains out, he rubbed my back and helped me take sips of water. What was wrong with him I thought to myself. I have never been treated so kindly like this before and it scared me, so I started to push away from him.

The next time we went out was one of the bad times, I was trying to keep up with him by drinking way more than my little body could handle. I weighed 105 pounds on my good day and he was at least 190 pounds, so he held his drinking way better than I could. I drank so much that night that I actually blacked out at the bar and knocked my head and bit through my lip when I fell down. We ended up fighting afterwards. It was clearly the alcohol that was the source for these unnecessary arguments and once again I was trying to push him away, but he insisted on working through this. It was almost as if he saw who I was deep down inside, even before I learned to rediscover that happiness myself.

Fast forward to a few years later, it was the night of his grandfather's viewing I had way too much to drink and I became this very ugly person. I had no idea what was happening, why it was happening or even how to stop it from happening. I got so intoxicated that I broke the window on our car, I tried to kick down the fence at the bar we were at, I got into a fight with some of his family members and apparently the cops were called on me. I don't remember any of this, and that scared the shit out of me. Who the heck was that person and where did she come from? My biological father is an alcoholic to this day and still drinks I feared that this was going to happen to me after that horrible night.

The very next day was my husband's grandfather's funeral, and I was not welcomed there. Honestly, I was extremely hungover crying at home wondering what the hell happened the night before and where we all went. Why was I not welcome and when would my husband be home? We had only been married for three months at the time, so this was definitely not a good start to our marriage. When Brad finally got home, he took one look at me and said, "It's either our marriage or the drinking." I needed to choose and that's all it took. I loved that man more than anything in my life. I knew that he was sent from GOD to rescue me, I just didn't understand why until that very moment. I quit drinking and I never touched another drop again. This past August, I celebrated ten years of sobriety. I never even attended any AA meetings or sought professional help. I did it cold turkey. I give that glory to God and with the love and support of my husband Brad. I believe wholeheartedly, that when you want something bad enough, when you LET GO and LET GOD, anything is possible to overcome; and your strength will rise above! I am UNMOVEABLE in my FAITH! If I hadn't quit drinking, my marriage would have ended and my youngest daughter would never have been born. Believe in yourself and watch the magic happen!

On my sobriety journey, I learned to love myself again, to accept my past and how to move forward. It's okay to not be okay, and it's okay to ask for help. You see, if I didn't go through this chapter in life, I wouldn't be where I am today, and I certainly wouldn't have the strength that I do now. The drinking days helped me grow, they helped me become a better version of me, and they helped me overcome what most people struggle to even admit that they have a problem with at all. I can admit now, that in those days, I had a drinking problem even though I didn't see it that way - nor did I want to see it that way. I was certain that I had my drinking under control until it was almost too late for me. GOD stepped in and he said, *"Enough is enough, child, I am going to help lift you back up and I am going to share your testimony to help give someone else hope."*

You see, we live in a world where many people are judging - including family members, and that's okay. Always remember, that shows a reflection of who they are, and NOT who you are. When we walk through these troubling days, we have already taken ownership of them and these mistakes. Therefore, we don't need to listen to anyone throwing them back in our faces or still looking at us like we are a bad person for what we have done in the past. Those people don't know what happens behind your closed doors. They don't see what you are going through. They don't see the tears; the prayers to God daily. They only see you for what they heard about you and that's okay. They don't walk in your shoes and therefore they can't take away your joy. We grow from these mistakes - and that, my dear friend, takes *strength and courage*.. Not everyone can overcome an addiction, so be proud of yourself and gosh darn it, I want you to shout it from the rooftop about how amazing you are!

Always remember how very loved you are.

Always remember that you are enough.

Always remember that you are deserving.

Always remember to be YOU!

Keep sparkling, keep shining, and keep smiling.

The world sees you and you are exactly where you are meant to be. Follow that calling darling, but when you do, make sure you do it with so much passion that you feel the burning desire in your heart.

Don't be ashamed of your story. You never know who needs to hear it and who you will help by sharing your voice with others. For many years, I kept silent on my past and it honestly was a block for me. That was stopping me from moving forward from the past. When we talk about our addictions and how they almost destroyed our lives, it helps open up the eyes to become sober and see the life that we were always meant to live. I am no longer living in shame of what I had done, as those days are gone. I am NOT that little girl who was once hurting so much that I was only trying to numb all those years of hurt, anger, sadness and pain. I am now someone who I am proud of. I am an amazing mother who has built her dream life with the help of God and my beautiful family.

I hope that you never stop believing in yourself and you find it within yourself to follow your heart to enjoy the ups and downs in this beautiful journey called life.

Looking through these Sober Eyes have been the best days of my life!

Reach out for help and if you see someone struggling, please let them know that there is hope.

ABOUT TABITHA SEEFELDT

Tabitha was born and raised in Sheboygan, Wisconsin. She moved to a small town called Oostburg the summer she was entering eighth grade, where her parents and brothers still reside. When she was seventeen years old she decided it was time to leave home and test her wings out. She is a firm believer in her faith and follows God's calling and lives life to her fullest. She is an avid book addict, a wife to her loving husband Brad and mom to her two beautiful daughters, Taliah and Bailee, along with a few heavenly angels. She is currently residing in Manitowoc, Wisconsin and enjoys helping others daily.

Behind closed doors, she struggled with the ghosts of her childhood scars, abuse issues, self-sabotage, anxiety and drinking. One day she woke up and decided that her life needed to really change and not just by quitting the bottle, she felt called to do so much more. She was determined to make a difference in her life. She believed that she deserved more in life. After searching to rediscover who she was for over a decade she has finally found her voice again and now she is working daily to help other women find theirs.

Tabitha works in the DS/MLM world and she got involved a little over eight years ago but never really committed to it until a few years ago when she found her fuel and burning desire to really make this work to better her life and her family's life. Tabitha believes in herself and knows that she CAN and WILL hit the Top of her company. Changing lives helping people find their Hope and Happiness again truly is her passion.

You can connect with Tabitha on the following platforms:

Facebook: https://www.facebook.com/tabitha.seefeldt.9

Facebook Group: https://www.facebook.com/groups/583570942008458/?ref=share

Instagram: @elev8edu

Email: elev8inglife2020@gmail.com

First Love Yourself

Kayla Daricek

I COULD FEEL THE HOT JUNE SUN BEATING DOWN ON ME through the thin fabric walls of my tent. "Mommy, Mommy, it's time to wake up!" my five-year-old daughter excitedly shouts at me from the campfire. The birds were chirping, and the slight breeze was gently rustling the leaves of the trees. It was a gorgeous summer day, but I was in rough shape.

Each time I moved, a sharp pain would shoot through my muscles and joints like a freshly sharpened dagger. My head was pounding. I was severely dehydrated, and that was no secret. The horrible feeling in my gut told me that something bad had happened the night before. Oh no, here come the sweat beads, my mouth is watering, stomach churning…yep, I was going to be sick. It started at roughly nine that morning and lasted until eight that evening. My first ever experience with alcohol poisoning, and it kicked my ass.

It did not take long for me to recall the events of the previous night, and they were not pretty. At the age of thirty-one I received my first DUI, aggravated at that, on the day of my daughter's fifth birthday. Something to be proud of, right? Not even close. The fact that I was facing legal trouble for the first time in my life completely devastated me, but it was not the hardest pill to swallow. The hardest realization was accepting the fact that I had wrecked my car into a guardrail and then having to own my truth surrounding my mental state leading up to this event.

Earlier that day, while sober and driving alone, the thought had crossed my mind to drive into the lake and say goodbye to the misery of my life. The thought alone scared me in that moment but having to accept that I had attempted it while extremely intoxicated took things to a completely different level. It was life-altering. I knew right then that I needed some serious fucking help and quickly, because this was not my first encounter with suicidal thoughts.

Many years prior, I was twelve years old. This was when the chaos and careless behavior began. I had been watching my dad battle severe depression and anxiety for three to four years due to an injury that he sustained at work and had resulted in his inability to return to the workforce. My parents began fighting quite frequently. Life at home was uncomfortable most of the time. One particular day, an ominous silence lingered throughout the house, to the point that I became worried about my dad, so I went to check on him. What I walked into… nobody could have ever prepared me for. There sat my father, in silence, shotgun barrel in his mouth. To say I lost my shit would be a complete understatement. Thankfully, my uncle and his wife lived close. I bolted out the door and straight over to their house, at which point law enforcement was contacted. From that point, things just got worse at home. In a fit of rage one evening, my dad grabbed me by my hair and tossed me across the room. At that point, I had enough. I moved out that evening, at the ripe age of thirteen.

I moved in with a great friend of mine for a short time and worked full-time while still attending high school. I also started partying a LOT! I looked forward to my weekends, because it was a promise of getting drunk and letting go of reality. My grades began to slip because of my careless lifestyle and the pressure of working a full-time job. I couch surfed for many years as a teen, landing wherever felt most comfortable. After months of frequent hospital visits and doctor's appointments, I was diagnosed with endometriosis at the age of fifteen. Due to so much missed school, it would have taken me an entire additional year of schooling for me to receive my high school diploma. With that being my only option, I dropped out. This was a decision that negatively impacted me for years to come. I lost a lot of confidence, focus, self-worth, appreciation, and the belief in my ability to complete important tasks.

With more time on my hands, I dove even deeper into dependence on alcohol. If I was not working, I was usually drinking. Although I maintained employment, by no means was I showing up as my best self, nor was I applying myself one hundred percent. Thank God for the bosses I had that showed me more grace than they should have. For many years, others saw far more in me than I ever saw in myself and looking back, I am so grateful for those who chose to voice their views and opinions of me, positive and negative alike.

At the age of sixteen, I experienced the toughest and most unexpected loss: my best friend Tyler. He was twenty-two and died due to a drunk driving accident that also claimed the life of another close friend of mine. Loss is hard, there is no doubt about that, and losing Tyler really shook my world. He had been my rock, my sounding board, my voice of inspiration, and my place of comfort for the last four years. Although he had served in the Army and spent a vast majority of the time I knew him stationed in North Carolina or fighting the war in Iraq, he and I spoke almost daily. He always made sure I was protected here at home. He cared, and he let it be known. Life without him did not make sense and alcoholism took over my life.

His passing taught me how fragile and short life really is. None of us know when today will be our last, so love hard, share your feelings, be authentic to yourself, and do not allow fear to stop you from ANYTHING! Feel the fear, but DO IT ANYWAY!!

For years, life was a roller coaster. At seventeen, I was brutally sexually assaulted and left as a disposable, used piece of trash on the side of the road in the town that I was born and raised. While hanging out with "friends" this one particular evening in the privacy of my own home, rufilin was added to my second beverage and what happened next is between "this man" and God. I will never know the full truth of what happened that night, just what I have been told, and I thank God for that. What I do know is I was left without clothing from the waist down, bleeding, and all alone. Luckily, I was found by some acquaintances trying to break into an auto body shop. I was screaming for my life out of terror. Again, by God's grace, I was not found by some predatorial stranger who could have had his way with me and I never would have known. Unfortunately, I was taken home and made to shower before being taken to the hospital, in hopes to remove all DNA or evidence of an assault occurring; this was done because these acquaintances were trying to protect the attacker and not me.

"So, although you can tell me who your attacker is and we know that the assault occurred, because there is no evidence to prove that it happened or who committed the crime, there is nothing we can do to help you," muttered the detective assigned to the case. While the assault did a lot of mental and emotional

damage, not to mention physical, the sheepish words of this detective stripped me of so much more. I lost my value, worth, self-love, and love for life itself. I felt like what had just happened was somehow justified in the eyes of others and by the law, but it destroyed me for the next thirteen years of my life. Little did I know that this assault would lead to PTSD, severe anxiety, self-sabotage, and hate. It completely changed my view on the world. I trusted no one for a very long time. My lifestyle became more careless than ever, and alcohol ruled my life more than I did.

In 2007, I was in a horrible motorcycle accident that resulted in temporary paralysis due to a dislocated pelvis and hyperextended spine (they actually told me that I would never walk again), and horrible road rash from the face down. A plethora of pain medication, nerve medications, and sleeping medications were prescribed just to get me through my days. This is where my first experience with opioid addiction started, and it reared its nasty head far quicker than I ever could have imagined. In 2009, at the age of twenty-one, another injury occurred that resulted in Complex Regional Pain Syndrome, a degenerative nerve disease; it is easy to say that I was prescribed opiates for a good three years straight as a part of treatment. This was also the second time that I was told that I would never walk again. When dilaudid was added to my string of medications to treat my nerve disease, the opioid addiction hit an all-time high and continued for seven straight months. Between alcoholism and opioid addiction, I was battling two very strong demons. God knew I needed a change even more than I did, but I just couldn't figure out how to escape the grip that these addictions had on me.

In 2010, I met the man that would become my husband. He had three children ranging from four to twelve years old: two boys and a girl. It was like a lightbulb went off in my brain and my life changed immediately. In July of 2010, I disposed of all my medications and quit taking them. My doctor told me that I could have killed myself by doing that, and while this true, what was most important to me was being a positive role model for the children who are now my bonus kiddos. I have always wanted to be someone they knew they could count on.

Our biggest downfall as parents was continuing to be severe alcoholics for the next four and a half years. I became an extremely violent drunk towards my husband; he is a man who has never laid his hands on me, even in self-defense. The violence came from the juxtaposition of spite and anger for not knowing how to walk away from alcohol yet knowing in my heart that my life was meant for so much more than to be an alcoholic. For this reason, my husband and I have broken up many times but our love has never allowed for a prolonged separation.

When I found out that I was pregnant in November of 2014, I was both extremely excited but terrified. I had been heavily drinking the weeks prior and all I could do was pray that my baby was okay. After extensive testing, they all came back perfect. After a very stressful pregnancy, we were blessed with a healthy, breathtaking, warrior girl on May 31, 2015. Everything that I thought I knew or wanted up to that point changed in an instant. My heart changed, and I knew that I needed to do better for her and for myself. For a while, I did. My focus was her, and any mamas that have breastfed know that that is a full-time job the first time around. Everything went great for the first three and half months, until my milk production stopped being enough to fill her up. I had to start supplementing with formula and it was not long before that was all she would take. I was devastated.

After being sober for a year, I went back to drinking to numb the pain of feeling like a failure as her mom. Fast forward to December 2015, and my violent tendencies returned while drinking. This time, my behavior led to my husband getting a restraining order against me out of fear and the need to protect his other children. The cops showed up to remove me and my six-month-old child. That was the lowest low of my entire life. My daughter had to stay with a friend for a few days because I had no idea where we going to go and I had to make sure she was safe while I figured it out. I was scared, I had failed my baby, and I needed some direction. I needed an idea of where to go from here. God was listening. He knew my heart and He knew what I needed to do. December 31, 2015 was the last time that I took a drink of alcohol, and I was certain that would last forever.

It did last for four and half years, during which time we had our son on March 11, 2019. Life was seemingly perfect. I was married to the love of my life, had one boy and one girl of my own, three bonus kiddos, and we were living in a place that felt like home for the first time since I was a young child. We had it all.

About a week after the birth of our son, my mind took a turn for the absolute worst. For days and days, I just cried for no obvious reason other than the nasty thoughts running through my mind. *"You are not good enough to be their mother. You are worthless. You are a failure to your family. They would be so much better off without your craziness."* This was the face of Postpartum Depression, and it was only the beginning. I was having such a hard time balancing the time between my newborn son, my four-year-old daughter, and my husband, let alone having any time for myself. For the first time in my life, thoughts of suicide swarmed by mind like a nest of angry hornets. When the thoughts began to form into plans to the point that I justified taking my newborn baby with me, I knew immediately that I needed help.

I was put on a serotonin balancing medication for a short time and had success with it. To this day I am unsure why my doctor at the time chose to take me off it, but that and my medical journey are for another time. I tried to get better on my own, without medication. Keeping myself busy was crucial. It left no time for the demons to manifest. I dove deep into my personal development journey, something that has changed my life in so many ways and that I continue to work at daily.

My downfall in my journey of sobriety came when I took a bartending job in August 2019. It was a gateway for me to reintroduce alcohol into my life, and one that I succumbed to in November. Things at home were extremely hectic, and those feelings of self-hate crept back in. It did not take long for me to start wanting the shots, wanting to party with "friends", and completely neglecting my duties as a mother and a wife. May 31, 2020, which was also my daughter's fifth birthday, was the day that God chose to show me how much of a disservice alcohol was serving in my life. Not only did I receive an aggravated DUI, but more importantly, I tried to end my life over false feelings and beliefs that I held about myself.

Thank God for the fact that He had other plans. I would have destroyed my family, leaving my children motherless and my husband without his life partner. It would have been a permanent solution to a very temporary problem. After waking up on June first and seeing the hurt and worry in the eyes of my family, I knew that my days of alcohol use had to be over.

I put myself into counseling that same week and have been going religiously every Wednesday since then. Personal development has hit an entire new level for me. I fill every free moment possible listening to podcasts, reading motivational books, connecting with people who are where I am headed in life, doing workbooks, and occasionally journaling. What I enjoy most is sharing my story with others in hopes of motivating and inspiring others to overcome the demons that may be holding them back. I want to help others realize the power that they hold within themselves to redefine and recreate their destiny.

The journey to self-love and appreciation has not been easy. In fact, it has been quite painful at times, but I can promise you this: it has been worth every tear, every breakdown, every harsh realization, and every minute that I have poured into myself. I will never "perfect" the process of self-love, but you will never see me give up. Shifting my mindset was the most important factor in me changing my life. I wholeheartedly love and appreciate who I am and all that has happened for me in my life, whether it be good, bad, ugly, or beautiful. Self-love is the magical key that will unlock the door to your soul's purest form of happiness, the kind that starts deep within and radiates through your eyes.

Rather than seeing myself as victim, I know I am a warrior and a survivor. I am strong, courageous, brave, tenacious, and fiercely loved. I am capable, worthy, and deserving of a beautiful life, and I am out to create it. My mission these days is to help others realize their VALUE, their WORTH, their STRENGTH, their ABILITIES, and help them to learn to fall in love with who they are, too. I strongly believe that people do not deserve to live a life where they feel like the world would be better off without them in it, because no matter what, that is not true.

No storm lasts forever, and a lot of beauty is found after the rain.

Choose life.

Choose love.

And choose to LOVE YOURSELF, ALWAYS!

Much Love,

Kayla Rae

ABOUT KAYLA DARICEK

Kayla was born in 1988 in Missoula, Montana. Raised in a small-town east of Missoula, she was privileged to attend school with many of the same peers from kindergarten into high school. Cherished friendships were created, many of which still exist today.

Kayla always enjoyed participating in sports. While softball was her all-time favorite, she was also fond of volleyball and basketball. On the evening of her freshman orientation, Kayla received a detrimental injury due to ego and careless behavior, which disallowed her to pursue any sports from that point forward. After becoming ill early in her sophomore year of high school, Kayla ended up dropping out of high school but completed the GED program at the age of 20.

At the age of 30 and after a fierce battle with Postpartum Depression, Kayla finally started on her journey of self-discovery, self-love, and everything in between. She will be the first to tell you that this journey has not been all rainbows and butterflies, but it sure is worth every moment that you pour into yourself.

Kayla is the proud and loving mother of two young children, ages five and one, and is also blessed with three incredible bonus kiddos as well. She is now on a mission to empower, uplift, motivate, and inspire people around the world to learn to love themselves wholeheartedly and without fault. She hopes to help people step into the truest and happiest versions of themselves that they have yet to even imagine.

"When you love who you are, happiness starts in the center of your core and radiates through your eyes. That is where the magic begins!"

-Kayla Rae

Kayla can be contacted at the links below:

kaylad0531@outlook.com

facebook.com/kayla.daricek2

Limitless

Shefali Chhabria

"GOOD AFTERNOON PASSENGERS. THIS IS THE PRE-boarding announcement for flight EK 501 from Mumbai to JFK. Regular boarding will begin in approximately ten minutes time. Thank you." This was the final call. I still had time to go back. What was I doing, migrating alone to a country I had only heard about? I kept thinking of turning back as my family was waiting outside the airport, in terror and fear of leaving their little girl alone out in this unknown world.

THAT day, when I boarded my flight with all my hopes and dreams packed in a bag, little did I realize the life changing experience awaiting me. Just a week before taking that flight, I was not fully committed to crossing seven oceans and living alone in a different world far from home. I had only one dream: FREEDOM. I kept visualizing the Statue of Liberty and kept thinking...I too can be free. Free from my problems. Free from limitations.

Growing up in a small town in India; I was raised with certain guidelines and limited beliefs.

"Girls are not supposed to work after college."

"Girls are supposed to be a vessel for making babies."

"Girls need to look a certain way or else they might get raped."

"Girls cannot have a love marriage, instead - they're 'assigned' a husband."

The list just goes on!

My curiosity and skepticism of the many guidelines I had to follow growing up allowed me to formulate my own perspectives rather than take things at face value.

One day, while sitting on a bench with my best friend, I began to tell her about my confined lifestyle.

She asked me, *"Why don't you think you deserve better? Why don't you apply for your Master's and plan to move to the States?"*

Despite being curious, these questions had never crossed my mind.

After witnessing most of my friends move to different places, all I could only repond. *"My dad doesn't let me out of my house after nine pm. How the hell will he let me go to a different country, especially the United States?"*

I laughed.

She said, *"If you truly believe you deserve it, you can achieve this. Take one problem at a time and don't confuse yourself being the 'problem'; make sure you know that you're the creator of your own destiny."*

Those words instantly pierced my heart.

The next day, I started preparing for my entrance exams to apply to universities in the United States. I was a software engineer working fifty hours a week, while spending four hours daily for my commute. I knew it would be nearly impossible to study alongside working, but I needed to continue to make this dream a reality. Just like all the other things in my life, I had to do this one way: SECRETIVELY. I built my dream with a pen and paper. I wrote down my goals and created a timetable just like I did to get top scores in my school boards. However, this was nothing like my school life. I had to wake up at six a.m. and learn some never ending list of vocabulary words on my way to work in a local train (which was nothing like the Path trains in New York). I had to stand and fight for my place in the passage of the ladies' compartments where I could smell every kind of sweat and what people had for breakfast through their breath every morning. I could hardly breathe in those moments; let alone have a book in one hand trying to read for my entrance exam. The only thing that kept me going was the smell of freedom. With all that was around me, I could still smell it and I knew it was my soul calling.

Fast forward, after several failed attempts, I got into some of my dream schools. I was nervous about telling my family that I had been accepted into prestigious universities in the States. I kept praying that this achievement would make them proud, but I understood they would need time to fully process it. They realized that I was adamant on leaving; regardless of whoever became the president of the United States. There was nothing that was going to stop me. I had a fire in me that kept sparkling and leading me towards my purpose.

The fire that was burning inside of me was hiding behind layers and layers of walls that prevented me from getting hurt. These layers acted as a defense mechanism, suppressing my fears of making decisions based on a single desire: freedom. I became numb to any love, empathy, and compassion.

This changed when I met Mohin, who was also going to the same university as mine in New Jersey. We took the flight to our dreams together. A seventeen-hour flight, which felt like nothing with him by my side. He was the complete opposite of me. He showed me his vulnerable side right from the moment we met. I kept teasing him for being such a sensitive, emotional freak who cried after watching romantic movies with unhappy endings.

Nevertheless, he was my person. He was my best friend. He was my family. He was my mom, my dad, and my brother all at once. He was everybody when I had nobody. Soon after, we took the same courses and lived nearby. We started dating. He pulled the emotional side out of me and I pulled his practical, tough side out of him. We both complement each other on such a deeper level that we used to eat and pray together. The more I stayed close to him...the more naked I felt; not physically, but emotionally. His eyes ran through to my soul. The level of intimacy we had was insane. We used to know what the other person was thinking just by looking at each other. We did have our differences and there were red flags (which always felt like red roses for us since the emotional intimacy was indescribable).

A year flew by with this guy...and felt like a day. Just in that year, I had changed as a person completely. I went back to India to visit my family. The feeling of seeing them after a mere year gave me chills. The day I landed, I felt like I was in a different place. I felt different. I felt like I had lost a year without them and I could not catch up to it all. I did not feel at home. There was a longing for belonging after becoming a NRI... a person with *No Rational Identity*. The only identity I was left with was: *my life was my karma*. It is a powerful saying from Indian origin; meaning whatever you do in your life, if your thoughts and emotions are in your control, you can make or break your life, either consciously or unconsciously. Before I could realize this, I hit rock bottom, both literally and figuratively.

It was Mohin's Birthday and I had recently lost my internship, so I was in no mood to celebrate, but I felt like I should at least get him his favorite lime-ariettas to celebrate. We had a couple of our friends over to celebrate and he got wasted by the time we ended our night. I was not drinking due to my period, but I enjoyed watching my friends getting drunk and having a laugh. As soon as the party was over, Mohin and I got into a fight. We both were angry, and I walked quickly across the hall since I was scared that he would hit me. As I said before, we say in India - *your life is your karma.* At that moment, I could have chosen to see the **divine** or the **devil** in him. The choice was mine and I chose the **devil.** The devil who had never hit a fly could possibly hit me. I made the wrong choice and that choice led to my downfall.

I slipped on the spilled lime-ariettas and fell flat on my face, all-while having one leg rotated in a 140-degree angle. I noticed blood between my legs as I started bleeding profusely due to stress from my period. Before I knew it, I was sitting there in the pool of my own blood. Thankfully, I was a big Grey's Anatomy fan, and I knew exactly what I needed to do next. I sat still on the ground, petrified, staring at my right leg. I closed my eyes sensing the energies of my guardian angels protecting my spirit and my mind from the pain. I felt the magic and it was sparkling around me like a protective shield. I looked at Mohin for help. I saw that he was completely unaware of the situation, as he was lying there drunk. I slowly dragged myself towards the bed and stretched my arms to get my phone and dialed 911. With a timid voice I told them that I was in no condition to move my body and I could hear my bones breaking with each passing second.

Just like that, the *"FREEDOM"* I came to find in the United States was tied into a plaster for months. I could not tell my family that I had been so reckless and irresponsible. I could not tell them I had turned from a runner to a person who may never walk again. I hid everything from them: from undergoing major surgery, to the number of screws and plates in my leg, absolutely everything. I still remember the day I was going to the operation room for the first time in my life without my family by my side, on 9/11. I had all the odd numbers stacked against me that day. It was the scariest day of my life. I wish I could tell you that everything was okay after my surgery, but the actual struggle began when I started my recovery. I was in a dark place for months. The only ray of hope was the love and care I was receiving from my person, Mohin. But even that was not enough since he was working twelve to fourteen hours a day. I was living by myself, enclosed in the four walls alone, and in a bed-ridden state for months.

One day, I was washing my hair under the bathroom sink with one leg up in the air when I thought to myself, *Is this what I deserve?* I saw a girl in the mirror crying for help. She wanted to give up. She wanted someone from her family to take care of her. She could not even manage to wash her own hair. I was scared to look her in the eye, as she was too weak and fragile. I kept avoiding that woman in the mirror for months, as she was telling me the truth I never wanted to hear. This was my rock bottom, the emotional one. I think the physical injury was quite small compared to the mental injury. After five months of bed rest, the day finally arrived when I was going to get rid of that plaster on my leg and start physical therapy.

As soon as I took my first step, I felt an electrical shock in my right foot and I could not put any weight on it, and I had to learn how to walk all over again. It took me eight months to reach a point where I could walk without assistance. I was limping for a very long time. When I asked my doctor for the time frame of when I would be able to walk normally again, he said, *"You might never gain full functionality of your leg. The limping might not go. You might have to reprogram your brain again...wiring it to not be scared of falling in order to reduce the limp."* I went through PTSD. Even inside my own home, I had to walk around with crutches due to my fear of falling.

It came to a point that I could not hide it from my family anymore. As soon as they knew what had happened, they booked me a ticket to visit them for a few months. I was the happiest when I flew back, I finally felt safe. I went for rigorous cupping and painful needling sessions along with electric shock therapy. It was painful, but my mom was mainly concerned about me not finding a husband due to my accident. So, she worked extra hard to feed me nutritious food to heal my bones. If only she knew, I did not need JUST my bones to heal, but also my **heart.**

My emotional healing began when Mohin left for DC to work, after completing graduate school. We broke up as his demons reflected mine and I knew I had to be **free** and do my inner work. I started walking without a limp soon after coming back from India, but I always felt limited. I felt like *"I am not supposed to wear heels. I am not supposed to run since I have implants in my feet. I am not supposed to go to the gym."* The rebellious kid in me started questioning things once again. I started smelling the sense of freedom again... achieving things that I CANNOT do.

I went out on my first date, wearing heels for the first time in two years. I took my gym membership and started working out. The more weight training I did, the more strength I gained. Before I knew it, I was running on a treadmill in a month's time. I was running as fast as I could with a fear of falling again along with the hope of rising again.

It took me years to understand how fascinating the human brain is. My doctor was right. I had to reprogram my mind to learn how to walk again, but not just that, I had to reprogram my mind to unbecome the person I was. You see, my journey all along was not about becoming something to achieve my freedom. It was about unbecoming the limited version of me. It was about removing those layers to be able to share my deepest and darkest secrets with you all. It was about being intimate and authentic with the people around the world, connecting with them through my story. The freedom I was looking for was not in running from my problems in India and creating new ones in the United States. Instead, The freedom was when I finally understood that there is **no** freedom at all. We cannot be free from our karmas, no matter where we go, we will have to pay for them. But while we do that, we can still be free in understanding that freedom is not something we can *have*, it is something we can *create* for ourselves.

We are living in a conditional world, Society does not give us the freedom to choose what we CAN and CANNOT do, even what we CAN and CANNOT become sometimes. Our physical world is made up of a limited belief system, but our internal world is *limitless*. We can have freedom to choose how to react, who we CAN and CANNOT become, what we CAN and CANNOT do.

After breaking and healing from my traumas and coming back to the light through those dark tunnels, there was a great love waiting for me. The love that helped me realize that the only freedom I have is the one that I create through my meditation. The place where everything is one, you and me, a space where I stop having any thoughts or emotions and reach a point of nothingness. **This** is the place where there is no judgement, only love and forgiveness, where nothing can touch us, not the limited belief systems or our **problems.**

This magical place helped me recognize the true meaning of gratitude and living in abundance. It helped me understand that we can achieve our desires through truly believing in ourselves. It helped me navigate the unconditional love I received from my family in the form of those stringent guidelines that were there only to protect me and not to suffocate me. All they wanted was to keep me safe and happy regardless of the immense pain they had to go through.

I cannot believe that I would be saying this, but breaking my leg was one of the best things that ever happened to me. It taught me to be thankful for little things in life and to smile at my struggles with compassion. It woke me up from a sleeping state that I was in for twenty-five years of my life. It helped me strengthen my faith in myself, and now instead of saying "Why me?" I ask myself - "Who else?" Who else has enough to get through this?

Who can emotionally navigate themselves through this better than I can? And this my friend, does not come from a place of ego; it comes from a place of self-love.

You came into this world with enough light to find a way out of the dark, enough strength to conquer every battle you are handed. Enough kindness to save a soul. Enough love to shift the planet, now why do you still worry? You are equipped with all the resources you could ever need. Look within, You, my love, you are drenched in magic.

In the cycle of karma...Be LIMITLESS by understanding the true power of GRATITUDE and INNER FREEDOM...THAT IS WHERE OUR MAGIC LIES.

ABOUT SHEFALI CHHABRIA

Shefali Chhabria is a poet, software engineer, animal-lover and now a co-author. Most importantly, she is a daughter of a proud and amazing woman, Harsha. She is passionate about helping and connecting with people to their fundamental core of their being. Shefali was born and raised in Maharashtra, India. She moved to States for her master's in information systems in 2019 from Stevens Institute of Technology, New Jersey. She has a great problem-solving mindset and is a sucker for analyzing human brain, people-science and reprogramming after years of programming for various IT Sectors. She is an avid gym lover, artistic, and free thinker.

She began her journey somewhere between living and dreaming, in New York city. On the core, she has always been a country girl who wears her shoes like slip-ons tied together with a smile wide across her face. Behind the scenes, she has been wrestled with some deep wounds of abandonment, suicide, health, and identity crisis. She appreciates her light after sitting with her darkness. Alone, in her stillness, she committed to becoming the woman who can help other women elevate.

Some of her great projects included enhancing accessibility features for visually impaired and blind users by developing sensors for the Contour Diabetes App. This application is used world-wide by diabetic patients. She helped in increasing the sales and usage for this application by making it accessible to people with special needs.

Shefali considers her spirituality as one of the core parts of her existence. She loves to express her love for the source through journaling, meditating, painting, and connecting with nature. She is learning to make meditation out of the mundane. Washing dishes, conscious cooking, and even while standing in the elevator by paying deeper attention.

She believes that the key part of our healing through hurt, trauma and dense conditioning can be achieved through going in-ward, self-love, learning to let go, self-awareness and building new habits.

You can connect with Shefali on the following platforms:

FACEBOOK:

https://www.facebook.com/shefali.chhabria

INSTAGRAM:

https://instagram.com/shefalichhabria

LINKEDIN:

https://www.linkedin.com/in/shefali-
chhabria-78015352/

Mirrors

Elizabeth Cirelli

66 THERE I WAS, LAYING PEACEFULLY ON MY BACK, *receiving a reiki healing. All of a sudden, the memories began to bubble up to the surface. The image was blurry, but soon came into clarity. The images were brighter and sharper. I could see an old white house and the street it was located on. There was a man with brown hair and a beard. Standing in front of him was a little five-year-old blonde girl. She looked precious and terrified, all at the same time. She also looked a lot like me. In that moment, I felt a rush of the feelings I had kept tucked away pulsate through me as they began to rise up and release out of me."*

You may have read my chapter in "She is Magic Too" called *Trauma to Triumph* where I spoke about my brain injury that had stopped me in my tracks and led me to a recovery process. It required me to be more still than I had ever been in my entire life. The world as I knew it: the hustle and bustle, the busyness, the planning and attending of events, the rushing from one errand to the next, all seemed to vanish from my existence overnight.

The amount of time I was spending with my thoughts, emotions, sensations, experiences, and profound changes within brought forward a thirty-five-year-old suppressed memory of sexual abuse. In the last book, I discussed the recovery process itself, but not the perspective it gave me after the rehabbing and healing were completed.

After I finished over fifty-five programs at The Kripalu Center for Yoga and Health, as well as the doctor recommended therapies, there was a stillness that I began to embody in this next chapter of my life. It took on a major role as I transformed into a new version of myself. Sitting with myself, honoring each moment, finding gratitude for what is, and diving into the mystery of life as it unfolds were all adaptations that took a lot of change and evolving before coming into fruition. Prior to the injury, I yearned for a more holistic career. I wanted less time working and more time enjoying life's pleasures. I wanted to be a published author and to find like-minded people. It was an inner conflict of wanting something different, but at the same time, not wanting to let go. I wanted things to change, but I was too scared to experience the unknown.

My mental health clients were such a big inspiration to me. In each one of them, I could always see some aspect of myself being reflected back, whether it was something beautiful, something not so pretty that needed tending to, or something that was locked down so deep that it might not be ready to start inching its way to the surface. As I began to set my sight on new horizons, I started writing a memoir for publication about a classmate I had gone to school with from preschool through the first year of high school.

The writing process was going well, until it wasn't. As my former classmate and I started to drift in different directions on the development of the book due to him having a hard time accepting the truths from his life, it simply wasn't working. I felt the Universe pushing back on the completion of the book. As I had for many years, I was resisting the push. At that time, I saw *resistance* as something you pushed against in order to keep *pushing forward.* I knew little about truly sitting still and listening to what the Universe was trying to show me or teach me. I thought, "Just keep pushing and you'll eventually get there!" What I hadn't learned yet was THE UNIVERSE ALWAYS WINS! So, I continued in my ignorance to push and to push. I was at such a loss as to why the book wasn't working that I actually talked myself into going to see a psychic. Now, let me be clear, visiting a psychic was absolutely NOT something I believed in. I was a "show me the facts" kind of girl. I needed them to be in print and proven!

But here I sat in this woman's home. I had written her off as crazy before she even started talking. I paid cash. I didn't want any record of me coming to see some whack-o about the future course of my life! Had it really come to this? Is this where I was seeking clarity? Had I lost all sanity?

She began by listening to me explain that I wanted to know what direction I should go with this book I had been writing.

"Is it a male?" she asked.

"Yes," I nodded.

"Does he have some sort of control over you?" She looked at me sternly.

"Ha! Yeah, right. No, not at all." I replied. I was a blissfully unaware control freak, so the thought of me letting some guy have control over me sounded hilarious.

She continued on, *"Does he have brown hair?"*

"No. He's bald."

"Well what color was it when he had hair?"

"It was a dark reddish color."

"I'm getting a rich, medium brown."

"Yeah, no. That's not him." I'm already feeling that this is a massive waste of my time.

"Are there any other men that have had control over you?"

"No. I've always had great relationships with men. Friends, family members, and people I have dated. To be honest, most of them have been quite overprotective of me in a good and healthy way."

I peered over at the clock wanting to dismiss myself early, but didn't want to be rude with an abrupt departure. A puzzled look appeared on her face, which then dissipated rather quickly.

"Ah!" she says, "You are supposed to be writing your own story, not his. And there is still some guy with some kind of control over you."

I force an appreciative smile across my face for the however many minutes I had left and thanked her as I am simultaneously spitting out thoughts in my head like, "What the hell was I thinking?"

It would be about a year later when what she had said to me would begin to make any kind of sense. It was seven months after that visit that I was met with a massive head injury. As I had started my healing work, memories began to surface. A few months after that, a chill came over me as I remembered what she had said to me. My memory during the reiki session involved a man with medium brown hair. My mind was spinning. *Was that crazy psychic lady right?*

As I sat there with one of my many journals lying beside me I thought, not only was she right about that man, but I've been recording my own story my whole life, journaling since I was in the third grade. *Was I really supposed to write my own story?* I *did* always dream of being an author. I thought back to the former classmate I had started writing a book about and pondered over my thoughts, knowing that everyone is mirroring something back to you. The abuse in his life had been a large part of his story. I didn't realize it at the time, but he was reflecting more back to me than I could have ever imagined.

We were incredibly different, so I struggled to see what we could possibly share in common. However, we did grow up in the same small town in Connecticut. As part of the writing process, we had journeyed together back to that same little town to help him recount his memories. He shared different stories as we whipped down various streets, passing our high school, the town library, making our way through the town center and then up past Northwest and Welch Park. I was listening to his story and at the same time quietly recalling my own memories of playing sports, attending birthday parties, pumpkin picking, going to Girl Scouts and hanging out with friends. While he was depicting his own memories of abuse, the Universe was gently nudging me back to the memories of my younger self, but they were too deep under the surface at that time.

I looked at my journals again, knowing how important it was to me to honor my inner child and give her back her voice. So, I grabbed one of the journals, cracked it open, and began to write. As time went on, I thought back about all the people who had shown up on this process at exactly the right time and what they were mirroring or reflecting back to me. I marveled at how it all seemed to make more sense four years later. Things just started to "click" as I revisited that moment of quiet stillness. I thought back to one of my earlier trips to Kripalu. I checked into my room like I always did: unpacking, putting my clothes into the various drawers, and awaiting the arrival of my roommate. Moments later, she appeared in the doorway. She introduced herself, explained what program she was attending, and that she was from just outside of Boston. She was cheerful and pleasant. I asked her what she did for work. She happily explained she was a speaker, as she was a survivor of childhood sexual abuse. I was admirable of her candid disclosure and at the same time, completely mortified! Who opens with that? But the synchronicity of it was too in my face for me to ignore. She too was my mirror, showing up at precisely the right time. She was the voice I needed to get back: confident, unashamed, and unapologetic.

The process of healing was up and down. There were moments that I could allow myself to feel things and shed what I no longer needed to carry. Then there were moments it still felt like it was all too much. The thoughts in my head were filled with, *"Will this ever end? Will I ever get my life back? I hate this! What's the point? What did I do to deserve this?"* I'm sure there were many more. I'm not sure how many months it took before the self-doubt, the questioning of everything and the pleading for it all to disappear eventually fell away. It was a process where I began to see that the difficult and confusing path was slowly providing me with everything I was asking for. I was just receiving it on different terms than how I originally imagined it. I was working less, which originally felt like a major loss. However, once I could shift my focus to see that as a positive result, I realized I was actually doing more of what I loved during the rehabilitation process. I was writing, practicing yoga and meditation, going hiking, doing stand-up paddle boarding, and kayaking. I was attending multiple yoga retreats and building my community of like-minded people. As I was attending these retreats, I was focused on the new friends I was meeting and the deep connections I was developing with them.

It wasn't until I attended a program with Lama Migmar, a Buddhist Chaplain from Harvard, that I realized even my greatest teachers were reflections of myself. I put them on such a pedestal that I couldn't recognize they were pieces of me, too. There was one moment when I stood outside of Kripalu with Lama Migmar and asked if him if he could possibly help me with a few things after the program was over. *"What kind of things?"* he asked. *"Ya know, like life?"* I said. He smiled, stood before me in his grounded and gracious presence, and calmly replied, *"I think I can do that."* He smiled and walked away. As he turned, I felt a rush of energy and my eyes began to well with tears. In that moment I realized the magnitude of his greatness and also the greatness that lived within myself. I sat down on the steps we had been standing on and watched his maroon robe fade off into the distance as he walked in the opposite direction. I thought about how almost nearly every teacher I had in the fifty-five programs I had attended had been authors, including Lama Migmar. It was within the next few weeks that I was introduced to my writing coach and started on my memoir.

It would be a year later when the majority of my head injury had healed, but aspects of my trauma still seemed to be lying within me. As I was visiting my parents in Colorado that year for Christmas, I reached out to an old friend I hadn't seen in about twenty years. He lived just five minutes from my house, and I knew from a Facebook post that he was home visiting his parents, too. I figured, why not? I sent him a quick message and we decided to meet up for lunch.

The most memorable moment I had of him as kids was when he hopped onto the hood of my car while we were in a parking lot. We were in transit, heading from one place to the next. As he was being a typical teenager and refusing to get off, I took my foot off the brake, allowing the car to roll forward. It was that moment that led to my first ticket! It's a little joke between us, but having the memory of the police officer seemed to play a deeper role in my reconnecting with him. While it might have been my first ticket, it wasn't my first interaction with a police officer. Also, while it was my friend's first interaction with law enforcement, it certainly wasn't his last. I was all too familiar at this point with people being brought into my life for a reason and no one showing up by accident. I knew in the back of my head the significance of this, but I was ready to be done with the healing! I felt like I had put in enough time. So, I brushed it aside and kept moving forward.

It would only take a week or two after returning home from my visit that I would be out driving around town and seeing an abnormal amount of police cars as I went from one errand to the next. As I gripped the steering wheel I let out an, *"Are you kidding me, Universe? Seriously?"* As I let out a sigh, another police car drove on by! I sat there convincing myself, *"Okay, okay…I will deal with it."* After I settled in for the night, I texted my friend. I didn't want to pry into his life…but at the same time, *I very much wanted to pry!* I basically wanted him to tell me that he never had a bad experience with the police and that I was just making up this whole *mirroring* thing in my head. So, half-prying into his life, I typed out via text, *"Have you ever been mistreated by the police?"* His response popped back up on my phone, *"Absolutely. Several times."*

While I had done a lot of work to heal the repressed memory of abuse, one component of it that I hadn't healed was that this individual was part of a police involved family. I can remember being five years old and watching my friend's dad enter the house during a play date. I remember seeing his uniform and the shiny gold rectangle glimmering with his name printed on it. I turned to her and said, *"Your dad's a police officer?"* She smiled and proudly replied, *"Yes!"* I looked over one more time and noticed the gun on his police belt. I was instantly frozen from fear, knowing the abuser had him on his side. It wasn't until my friend from high school and I sat in a Skype call with each other, bantering over politics related to gun owner rights with his gun sitting beside him, that I was able to connect the dots between my beliefs around this issue and the experience that impacted it. The vision of the gun on the police officer's belt flooded back to me; in that moment I realized that my memories from so long ago had been shoved in the back of my brain to be remembered at a time that would be deemed safer. My friend from Colorado was yet another mirror for me, helping me to continue down the path of healing.

I am so grateful for all of the people who have showed up on my journey. I truly believe everyone has a story that matters and some aspect of it sheds light on someone else. After I continued to heal the remaining part of my trauma, I had a sweet friend from Kripalu reach out to me and say, *"Hey, do you want to be a part of this book with me where a group of women all share their story of resilience and healing?"* And there it was again: a collision of precisely the right timing. I excitedly accepted the offer and had a wave of nerves come over me until the release day of the book because I didn't know how it would be received; it was that unsettling feeling of the unknown. But to my surprise and excitement, it hit the #1 Amazon Best Seller list and the International Best Seller list. That, ladies, is how you make a comeback!

You dig deep.

You surround yourself with amazing people and you give gratitude to all the people who showed up and supported you, lifted you up, and reflected pieces of you to get you where you were meant to be!

ABOUT ELIZABETH CIRELLI

Liz was born and raised in Windsor, Connecticut and moved out west to Colorado during her teenage years. After graduating high school in 1996, she attended the University of Northern Colorado, Colorado State University, and also obtained her Aesthetician's License at Cosmetology School. She moved back east after completing her undergrad studies and later completed her Masters of Education in Counseling Psychology through Cambridge College in Massachusetts. She enjoys warm weather and spending her time outside doing anything from hiking, kayaking, hanging out at the beach, camping, watching the sunset, and staring at the stars. She also enjoys the company of great friends, practicing yoga, meditation, and going out to eat. She is married to her loving husband Mike, has an older brother, and loves her little niece and nephew more than words could describe. She currently resides in Manchester, New Hampshire.

Liz spent 18 years in the Mental Health field working as a Licensed Psychotherapist in various agencies and private practice. She also held her School Guidance Counselor Certification and worked in schools as well. She specialized in working with individuals struggling with the impacts of trauma, anxiety, and depression. Liz has worked with children as young as the age of 4 all the way through adults 65+. She managed a heavy caseload while also collaborating with doctors, courts, probation officers, and school officials so her clients received the best well-rounded treatment she could provide for them.

Liz eventually left the mental health field and set her sights on more holistic practices to build upon her already large wealth of knowledge and expertise. She became trained as a Certified Yoga Teacher, Master Level Reiki Practitioner, Meditation Teacher, and Life Coach. She currently runs her own company, Elizabeth Cirelli Holistic Services, and is currently taking clients. She recently got back to writing, which had always been a childhood passion of hers, and has co-published her second book with Blair Hayse Publishing. In addition, she has recently accepted a Sales Representative position with Blair Hayse Publishing! She continues to focus on her personal memoir with hopes to publish it in the future.

You can reach Liz through her website www.elizabethcirelli.com or at www.psychologytoday.com

Or connect with her via email, phone, or Facebook:

ewoodrow2@yahoo.com

978-710-9598

https://www.facebook.com/liz.woodrow.18

1000-Piece Puzzles

J.P. Fourie

I TOOK A PREGNANCY TEST TWO WEEKS BEFORE MY SWEET Sixteen and it came back positive. I was a virgin.

My appendix had ruptured and in order to operate, a pregnancy test had to be administered. Hours passed as I tried to convince the doctors and nurses that I was a virgin. It wasn't until my parents ordered them to operate that I was finally rid of the excruciating pain. I fell asleep knowing I had appendicitis and woke up to learn that I also had a malignant tumor the size of a grapefruit attached to my left ovary. My hormones were all as true, and that's what had caused my positive pregnancy test.

The surgeries, loneliness, fear, bulimia, and addictions that followed were an absolute beast. My longing for any control over my illness set me searching for control in other ways. I wanted nothing to do with any memory of being sick. I did not embrace the fight, nor did I admit to myself that I needed outside help. My sixteen-year-old self-got back in the water and swam, not realizing I was close to drowning.

The days, months, and years following my diagnosis were nothing less than fuckery. When I should have been in counseling, I instead found myself following music around the country and living carelessly with no discussion of my illness to anyone. I powered through high school and university with great grades and graduated with two bachelor's degrees. The path that was expected of me was to find a teaching job and begin my career. Instead, I moved to the Caribbean with my small dog and a duffle bag. It was there that I was able to begin to focus on myself.

Perhaps some people would consider this running away from my problems. I found it to be liberating, and my definition of selfishness no longer carried a negative tone to my ears. I had to be honest with myself and no longer listen to the shit talk whirling in my head that I had created or others had imposed on me. Being alone and feeling lonely are two very different experiences. Now I had no one I knew around me, and I began to feel more connected with myself. I taught at the local university and bartended around the island. No one besides myself determined my next step. My healing had finally begun.

I found healing by swimming, dancing, teaching, reading, traveling, and simply standing still. Time spent by myself became more common and I gravitated inwards, recognizing the years of mental and physical pain I had placed upon myself. It was just me I had to care for, until the day came when I was asked to guard someone's heart.

It was a full moon in 2003 when I met my soulmate. He remains to this day my rock (or shall I say boulder) and with him I live a life of love and chaos. To find love when I least expected it taught me that our hearts are truly a muscle and that they can become stronger if you allow it to workout. I didn't want a relationship and yet his mind, soul, and touch would not escape me. I guarded his heart the best I could at the time and eventually caught him, never letting go.

Relationships come in all different forms. At sixteen years of age, I began my relationship with cancer. Sixteen years later, I fell into a depression so deep that I had to fly off the island and seek medical help. Simple tasks became unbearably complicated, and I often found myself sobbing in a dark room without knowing why. One year later, I was diagnosed with breast cancer.

My reflection of the previous sixteen years of my life helped me fight the second cancer diagnosis. Those years prepared me to fight breast cancer in a much healthier and conscious path. I was thirty-three years old, married, and had a four-year-old son when I was diagnosed with my second bout of cancer.

December 21, 2012 marked the end of an era on the Mayan Long Count calendar. The Mayans (and many individuals) believed that December 21st would reset the date to zero and signal the end of humanity. Many of us heard it being called "Doomsday." That day marked the beginning of a long and difficult fight.

It felt like someone had taken a lighter and lit it against my right breast. I immediately began to feel around and felt the tumor. The movie my husband and I were watching quickly became a horror as I profusely sobbed in his arms. The following morning, we went to see my doctor who then sent me for an ultrasound and mammogram. The result came back with two "masses" in my right breast and the doctor made me promise that if I needed any further treatment, that I would not seek it out on the island. Three days later, my family and I were on a plane heading north for Christmas and a meeting with the breast surgeon.

The room was as sterile as they come. My husband sat in front of me as the surgeon performed the biopsy. As she was finishing, I looked over and asked if she thought it to be cancer. Her simple and premature response was, "yes." The pathology report would come back in three days to confirm the diagnosis. Upon reaching my parents' home, I sank into the couch hoping that I was going to wake from this nightmare.

I found myself quickly reassuring my family and friends that everything was going to be okay. In all honesty, I was only trying to convince myself.

Doomsday came with my breast surgeon calling to inform me that it was indeed breast cancer. My first and only question was if it was treatable. Her response was *"Don't worry. You aren't going to die before Christmas."* That was the last time I ever heard her voice.

Christmas came and our son received the scooter of his dreams from Santa. Not knowing my fate or even if my cancer was treatable, I took in every moment as though it could be my last. I kept asking my husband if we were still living in this nightmare.

The New Year has always been one of my most favorite times of the year. It represents new beginnings and a great excuse to party! My husband and I took the train to New York City for an amazing dinner and concert with close friends. I was re-energized by seeing them and played that moment over and over in my head later on in my fight. We danced, laughed, and smiled throughout the entire concert. I felt the energy from the floor up. It was the only three hours since my diagnosis that I didn't hurt, struggle, or fear. I was able to escape and let only the music fill my head. Bob Marley says it best, *"One good thing about music, when it hits you feel no pain."*

The first two weeks of 2013 were an abundance of meetings with doctors. My oncologist decided to treat me as aggressively as possible. Being that my cancer had an estrogen receptor, it was called Her2/neu Positive. It was believed that my cancer was caused by the hormones I began taking at sixteen after both my ovaries were removed due to malignant tumors. I was then told to stop taking my hormones, which then put me in a medically induced menopause. This was my second time going through menopause, but it felt like a breeze compared to everything else going on.

January 14th was when I began my first of sixteen chemo treatments. My emotions were scattered and I felt so overwhelmed. All I wanted was to wake up from this nightmare. I drove down to the hospital with my husband and mother on Monday morning to receive my first infusion. This was the beginning of MANY treatments and doctor's appointments, all of which The Three Musketeers (myself, husband, and mother) attended together. The support I received from my two fellow Musketeers was, and still is to this day, indescribable. Honestly, I am unable to put into words the support, love, and compassion I felt from both of them.

I met with my oncologist before my first treatment. He described the medications and once again, drew more pictures of the breast, and explained my odds and the plan of attack. Then, he introduced me to Bonnie. Bonnie is an angel on earth with a foul mouth and a sense of humor that can take your mind off of anything. She is the perfect chemo nurse, one who I quickly built a close bond with. She always got me a private room for my infusions and even gave me her private cell number to reach her. She knew the ins and outs of chemotherapy, steroids, and all the side effects that came with them. As I took my anti-anxiety tablet, Bonnie hooked me up and I began my first chemo treatment.

A lot of people assume that hair loss is one of the most difficult parts of chemotherapy. For me, it was one of the easiest. My hair began to fall out exactly two weeks after my first treatment. I got it cut short to make it less dramatic, and when my pillow looked as though it had a life of its own, my mother and son shaved my head. Standing in front of the mirror with my son, I realized that it's how you say things that can make a huge difference between understanding and sorrow.

Waiting in multiple waiting rooms took a toll on me mentally. I was always the youngest by at least twenty years and received looks of pity. The casual shaking of the head or lopsided smiles made me feel like I was too young for this illness. Rather than feeling sorry for myself, I often listed things in my head that I was grateful and privileged to either have or had experienced. I would see my family and friend's faces in my mind and I would take myself back to memories of laughter as I sat there in those waiting rooms.

I was surrounded by family and friends and yet, I had never felt so lonely. I was in a daze and felt like I was never going to get out of it. Time felt like eternity and I wanted to sucker punch anyone who told me to *"think positive."* Between New Year's and my first chemo treatment, I also needed a LEEP procedure which removed part of my cervix due to pre-cancerous cell growth. I grew tired, alone, and overwhelmed.

The side effects of chemotherapy were at times extreme and consisted of: bone pain, hot and cold flashes, headaches, fatigue, nausea, constipation, dizziness, water retention, swelling, neuropathy, a burning sensation on my upper back, anxiety, and fear (sounds like a drug commercial, I know). I was put on six different nausea pills and steroids. I became anxious about all the drugs in my system and felt that my body was becoming toxic. I substituted more than half of the nausea pills with medicinal cannabis. Upon doing so, the nausea subsided, I slept better, and gained a great appetite.

I kept myself busy with my little man and 1000-piece puzzles (we completed five). We experienced a huge blizzard which I had looked forward to and my husband cooked some amazing food. During this time, I became neutropenic, couldn't have people over to the house, and at times had to even wear a mask around my own family. I still wasn't waking up from this nightmare!

Sixteen rounds of chemotherapy finally came to an end and a double mastectomy was to follow. However, this is where the details of my illness stop for the time being.

What I find to be most important and magical is the awareness I developed during these difficult times. I grew. I changed. Most importantly, I believe that I am not defined by these experiences. I am not defined ever. I am constantly changing, and therefore the definition of who I am is constantly changing. My experiences have helped shape me, sure. However, it's how I deal with my experiences that define me more than the experiences themselves.

We all live within magic.

Either we acknowledge it or not; that is our choice.

I choose to believe.

ABOUT J.P. FOURIE

J.P. Fourie was born and raised in New England. Her travels have led her to Uluru and the study of Dreamtime, cage diving with great white sharks, tall ass buildings, rainforests and tree houses, Machu Picchu, cobblestone pathways, and an amazing beach bar. She is currently busy mastering the moonwalk and is constantly in awe of her two humble and intelligent children. Her husband still can take her breath away and swimming is her therapy. She holds two bachelor degrees in anthropology and secondary education. J.P. mostly listens to reggae music, will put cilantro on anything, and collects crystals.

J.P. Fourie is nervous as hell to share her story. Her hope is that her words will help guide someone who is struggling.

You can email her at: choosetobelieve44@gmail.com

Coming of Age with Cancer

Jennifer Kirch

**With age comes wisdom,
with cancer comes strength.**

As of the publishing of this book, I just hit the milestone birthday of fifty. As a young woman, looking at fifty in the distance, I saw my life completely differently. I visualized my happy family; however, the Universe had other plans for me.

I never imagined that stage IV metastatic breast cancer would be detected at forty-seven. News which would forever change every aspect of my life. In the almost thousand days that I have been diagnosed, I've done my absolute best to be optimistic, positive, and consider myself a thriver. Throughout this journey, I learned to find my voice, and it's time to let cancer know the lessons learned through this fifty-year old's lens:

Dear Cancer,

Thank you for waking me the hell up.

I'm even more grateful that intuition got through to me first and gave me the necessary guidance to train in Mindfulness, Meditation and Yoga to give me the tools so that I could truly learn from you.

It's with gratitude that you allowed me decades of knowledge before you presented yourself. Although with these older eyes, I am aware now you were silently building up for years when I didn't know what I now know.

In my twenties and thirties, busyness was a badge of honor. Sticking with what I thought worked, that continued into my early forties.

Being a teacher trying to get by on a single income required me to spend my summers waitressing, tutoring, working at a winery, golf course, retail stores, plus numerous interesting jobs along the way to pay the bills.

It took until your vice grip on my skull which was mistaken as a horrific migraine to bring everything to a screeching halt.

This is where you made your grand entrance. No small lump, you presented yourself in your fullest form.

Finding out that you not only were stage IV breast cancer, but you had metastasized into my skull.

Lesson learned:

The skull protects the brain and the hippocampus which strengthened my belief in the importance of memory and learning. You humbled me beyond words, as this fervent reader now had difficulty reading, spelling and processing every day thoughts due to chemotherapy and radiation treatments to my skull.

This made me become a better teacher to my students, because what previously came so naturally my entire life, now required extra hard work. It provided a deeper understanding of those who struggled or didn't do work ~ possibly because they couldn't or were simply too overwhelmed.

My proudest moment fighting radiation and chemo-brain was crossing off a bucket list goal of earning my Yoga Nidra certification at Kripalu, thanks to a dear friend supporting my dream.

Although there were so many classes and exciting experiences offered, I politely thanked my sangha for including me, but went back to my room to study. Each night involved rereading chapters three to five times to comprehend, which allowed meeting with success due to motivation and determination. (I'm elated that two of these magical women from my sangha are also sharing their stories in this volume.)

Humbled beyond belief - a vivacious reader my entire life and an English teacher nonetheless, from July 2018 through March 2019, I struggled with reading comprehension. It took until truly wanting a goal for years where I was able to "get over myself" and get past my ego to be able to read, reread, reread, and so on until meeting achievement.

My fifty-year-old eyes smile back at the parallel memory of wanting to read so badly at age three. My parents were both educators and my sister was two and a half years older than me. For the first time, my Pop Pop (my maternal grandfather), gave my sister a present and in my toddler mind, *it wasn't even her birthday!!* It was this amazing Snoopy lunchbox, and oh how I loved Snoopy! Seeing my sad face, my Pop Pop said, "When you learn to read and you go to school, you can have one, too." I took him quite literally. Having a November birthday, the district we lived in wouldn't accept me into Kindergarten, and I was determined to go to school. After all, I was already four and I had learned to read. Driving my mother nuts, I wound up enrolled in the Hebrew Academy. Alas, no Snoopy lunchbox for all my efforts, but my lifelong passion for learning and knowledge began.

This also influenced the importance of coming to terms with memories pre-cancer and provided a deeper appreciation of my experiences with people after being diagnosed.

So, skull cancer, lesson learned.

But, you didn't start there. You originated in my right breast, and quite aggressively, I might add.

Lesson learned:

The right side symbolizes male energy. I spent the majority of my life looking for what I thought I "should have" or what I thought I needed. I was stuck on the societal norms of having a husband before buying a house or a child and these norms became so important to me.

I didn't have the confidence, self-love or knowledge in my younger years to know that you don't need to "settle" in order to settle down. Like Dorothy, I had the power all along.

My very first treatment was hormone therapy, in which artificial menopause was during chemotherapy.

In my previous chapters, I spoke about how I saw myself with my own family, house, more stability and, most importantly, healthy.

In college, one of my sorority symbols was a strawberry (actually Zeta Tau Alpha is a women's fraternity). I had many side gigs ~ and one was working for a friend at an educational toy store in Princeton. They had the sweetest doll in a strawberry dress that I purchased and quietly put away in my parents' attic for my future daughter. I've never mentioned this to anyone before, and I'm not even sure that my parents know this precious doll is still there.

I truly struggled with you here and the thought you had robbed me of that future.

When it was time to get rid of you, at least in my breasts, my surgery was switched in the operating room, and instead of the bilateral mastectomy that was non-negotiable for me, I came home with a single mastectomy. I wasn't given any time to prepare mentally or emotionally for how my body would look physically.

Grateful that your original site was FINALLY out of my body, I felt disfigured to my core. On top of that, chemotherapy caused my long red hair to fall out. What kind of woman was I now? Looking in the mirror was beyond difficult.

Oh, how I longed for the teenage years and my twenties, where I thought my body was "less than perfect."

Loving fashion was always a part of my nature. Having formative years in the Eighties included having Aussie Sprunch sprayed hair that was its own separate entity and wearing baggy Esprit, Benetton, and Au Coton clothes that covered up any curves.

If only I knew then what I know now…

My chest and hair were a large part of my identity as a woman. Once you ripped them away from me, I had to rethink the essence of femineity. I found other aspects of myself that made me feel feminine - grace, style, my smile and the way I carried myself.

Since the breast is an organ that provides nourishment, the problem with my breast was also symbolic of the fact that I stopped nurturing myself a long time ago. This realization empowered me to make changes that I was afraid to make for many years. I made changes at home, carving out time for yoga, art, crafting, learning new skills and other interests, which I "couldn't" find time for before.

Always diving into fashion trends, I quickly figured out how to select outfits to easily conceal medical devices or effects of operations. I grounded myself in meditation daily and repeatedly reminded myself that I am not my physical body.

Stage IV Metastatic Breast Cancer, lesson learned.

You metastasized all along my spine causing chronic pain.

Lesson learned:

Well, Cancer, you literally gave me a backbone, confidence, and the ability to stand up for myself.

The skeleton supports us physically, and ends up being analogous to metaphoric support. The muscles may represent strength, but the skeleton ultimately provides a conduit with which to exert that strength. You cannot move others without a foundation that you yourself stand upon.

In researching Chinese Medicine, the spine and bones' negative emotions are represented by symbols of power, authority, and fear.

Almost my entire life, I never stood up for myself. Looking back on every decade, there are examples of me being afraid to rock the boat, following directions to a fault, and being afraid to say anything controversial.

However, my first-grade self didn't have all of these limiting beliefs. Freshly out of the Hebrew Academy, public school was extremely different. Before the holidays, I remember walking through the hallway with my class to the cafeteria. Looking at all the Christmas trees and Santas, something compelled me to step out of line when I saw the principal. Never mind that she was in the middle of disciplining a child in the hallway. With wide eyes I sincerely asked, "Where are the dreidels and menorahs?"

I would love to sit down and talk with my first-grade self and learn at what point she was silenced and afraid to step out of line. *Whether it was standing up to you, Cancer, dealing with insurance denials, or even larger issues - I have found my voice, lesson learned.*

As you metastasized throughout my bones, you killed part of my jawbone and more.

Lesson learned:

Really, Cancer?!

Xgeva injections were a part of my treatment regimen from day one which were supposed to help strengthen my bones where you metastasized throughout my body. Later, I found out that this drug caused a portion of my jawbone to die, cracking a tooth from the inside and I already had some tongue paralysis.

Additionally, radiation treatments cause extreme dry mouth. Symptoms include difficulty in speaking, eating and swallowing, altered taste sensation, and malnutrition.

I've spent most of my adult life being a foodie, knowing incredibly talented chefs and enjoying some phenomenal wines discovered both from my parents' worldly travels and my sister and her family living outside of San Francisco for years.

My diet changed dramatically to take you on… no wine, no ice cream, honestly… no favorites. Today, I eat almost all organic and mostly plant-based foods, but many times food is not appetizing.

I'm still learning from you... I found my inner voice on a larger scale. I began to blog, speak up and out to help other oncology patients, and something I never imagined in a million years, I am an International Bestselling Author twice - *(I'll even pull my best David Rose and dare say thrice!)*

The mousy me of my younger years would never expose myself so candidly. I am honestly thankful, grateful, and blessed for that. *I learned to speak up and out, even through maxillofacial surgery and side effects - lesson learned.*

You maneuvered yourself into my right hip and pelvis causing difficulty with standing and walking.

Lesson Learned.

Almost every yoga class that focuses on the hips likes to refer to them as the "junk drawers" of the body and how emotions are stored there.

Hip problems relate to fear of going forward in major decisions - perhaps, the fear that there is nothing to move forward to. Interestingly enough, this did not occur to me until well into my diagnosis.

It could have easily been resistance to my current experience. This occurred after my long-awaited reconstructive surgery was cancelled due to your coming out of remission and during Covid, so it made perfect sense timewise.

This was the first-time allowing anxiety and fear to enter the picture since you've been my teacher.

Concerned about my life purpose, feeling insecure and standing on shaky ground, I felt fear moving forward in life, career and relationships. I didn't know at the time what needed to change, and that resulted in a fear of the future.

My undergraduate degree is in Sociology and Psychology. Helping others always aligned with my life's purpose. I originally wanted to go into clinical Social Work, but interviewing with different graduate schools, I was told I had no life experience. That September, I went back for a Masters in Arts and Teaching and have spent the past twenty-six years in public education. Socio-Emotional Wellness has always been important to me, and for years my passion has been trying to create this as a full-time position.

To keep my positivity up, I read Louise Hay's affirmation on my mirror daily: "I am in perfect balance. I move forward in life with ease and joy at every age." *No matter what, I stand firmly in my life's purpose. Hip cancer - lesson learned.*

Your aggressive nature was truly invasive of my lymph nodes.

Lesson Learned:

These small bean-shaped structures are part of the body's immune system. They help filter substances that travel through the lymphatic fluid and they contain white blood cells that help the body fight infection and disease.

According to Louise Hay in *Heal Your Body,* "Lymph problems are a warning that the mind needs to be recentered on the essentials of life: love and joy." In my last chapter, I spoke to this with cooking, singing and the Ho'oponopono prayer. *Cancer in the lymph nodes, lesson learned.*

You moved into my lungs.

Lesson Learned:

Multiple nodules showed up in scans of my lungs. Most recently, I have been accumulating fluid here which causes me to get winded easily and, oftentimes, have difficulty in breathing. Twice, I've needed procedures done to remove fluids.

Your message is loud and clear. I see life with lenses of gratitude, love and hope. Miracles are seen daily.

When you enter the lungs, it often relates to the inability to take in life. Grief and sadness are often related to the lungs. As much as possible, I keep a smile on my face; however, you can wear me down. I do miss many aspects of my old life and needed to allow time to grieve and let go.

At seventeen, a drunk driver rear-ended me, and hospital x-rays showed a small nodule on my lung. For years, I needed yearly scans to ensure that it never changed shape or size. *All of these years, the one nodule remained the same, until now. Lesson learned, lung cancer.*

I felt amazing this summer going for scans… didn't expect to see you much at all. I felt this with every fiber of my being. In all of your splendor, fifty - yes - fifty new nodules appeared in my liver.

Lesson Learned:

Problems with the liver are usually associated with a fundamental denial of one's value, anger, and primitive emotions.

There is only one remedy — compassion. I know I am doing my best, and need to allow myself grace. When you had me dig down deeply for the primitive emotions, I uncovered that I felt, at times, I am a burden on my parents, aging them prematurely.

A teacher once said to me, "When you heal the present, you heal the past and future, too." I've discovered the truth of her wisdom. Healing is not linear. When a wound is healed, it is healed through time and space.

When we allow ourselves to experience complete love, there are no more concerns about achievement or failure, or the value of your life, because those concerns exist in the friction of our thoughts and emotions. When you surrender to the healing antidote of love, all that there will be is love. *Liver Cancer - lesson learned.*

Cancer, I can handle you, you've taught me volumes. However, adding Covid confinement is a cruel addition.

You were the wakeup call for me to change my life so that I would no longer be unhappy. Additionally, you were symbolic of my spirit screaming that I wasn't truly happy, but you empowered me.

You provided the courage and impetus to make changes that people usually don't make out of fear or apathy — like resolving a long-standing conflict with someone or pursuing a dream that has become crushed under the weight of an unfulfilling life.

Thank you, Cancer, for your lessons to help me cope. I'm going to use these to help me deal with the latest plague, Covid. Dealing with you is stressful enough on a good day, but when you factor in the stressors of job uncertainty, social distancing, and life-threatening disease - the strength you've given me becomes indispensable.

At this age, and with this newfound wisdom, you have given me the power to get through anything. Looking at my life in review after fifty years, I am content in the knowledge that I am surrounded by close friends, a loving family, and the memories accrued during this lifetime.

Getting can was truly a blessing in disguise for my life. I am happier and more fulfilled today. As a friend said recently, it was how I chose to handle my journey with cancer that allowed me to step into my magic.

I am nourished with the wisdom that I have gained, the strength that will get me through this, and the memories that I will forever cherish.

"Aging is an extraordinary process where you become the person you always should have been."

~ David Bowie

ABOUT JENNIFER KIRCH

Jennifer grew up outside of Ocean City, NJ. She attended The College of New Jersey, formerly known as Trenton State College, for both undergraduate and graduate studies. She received her BA in Sociology and Psychology in 1992 and her Masters of Arts in Teaching in 1994.

Upon graduation, the lure of living at the beach brought her back home. She's been a public-school teacher since 1994 teaching all subjects in elementary school and English in middle school.

Jennifer loves her community and proudly supports small businesses. She enjoys fashion, learning, reading, travel, yoga and meditation.

A certified yoga and meditation teacher, she thrives on learning more about mindfulness, meditation, numerous healing modalities, and how-to bring socio-emotional wellness to others.

Diagnosed with stage 4 metastatic breast cancer in May of 2018, Jennifer has inspired many with her healing journey. She is blessed beyond words and forever grateful for her family and friends who have created an army of support and love like no other.

Jennifer is the founder of Pause and Reflect Yoga, LLC, and The Warrior's Voice Blog.

This is the third time she has shared her magic with the She is Magic series, and is forever grateful for the opportunity of becoming an International Bestselling author alongside so many incredibly inspiring women.

She shares her home with the beautiful Kwan Yin, a Maine Coon rescue who is extremely outgoing, lovable, and healing beyond belief. Luckily, this feline lives up to her namesake - the goddess of loving kindness, compassion, and healing.

To connect with Jennifer:

Facebook: Pause and Reflect Yoga

Instagram: jmk_pause

Website: pauseandreflectyoga.com

Email: pause.and.reflect.yoga@gmail.com

Four Moments
of Awakening

Chloe Evans

*"You are braver than you believe,
stronger than you seem, smarter than you think, and
more loved than you will ever know."*
– A.A. Milne

IN LIFE, THERE ARE MOMENTS THAT CHANGE THE WAY YOU think and exist forever. I have had many moments that have shaped me into the woman writing this chapter, sharing with the world what is on my heart and mind. I want you to know that you can dream your dreams and have them too. Being a writer has always been a dream of mine, and here we are. I share this with you to inspire you. Every moment is an opportunity. Yet, if it were not for the moments I share with you in this chapter, I may have missed the truth of what I value and aspire for in life. For me, the meaning in life has come down to feeling passionate about my life, the people in it, and keeping joy, hope and inspiration as the fire that fuels the legacy of love I hope to leave behind.

How do you find the courage to step up to your life, reclaim your power, ignite your passions, and build a legacy you love?

You take care of the moments.

Moment 1: The moment I remembered who I was and where I came from.

"You are responsible for doing what makes you happy," my grandma cut me off.

I was stunned. Not that my grandma had cut me off, but that she had said it at all. My grandma had dementia and it slowly stole her away from us before her body did. Now, on our calls together, she listened quietly as I shared stories reminding her who I was and our memories together.

Before dementia, my grandma was a no BS type of woman with an unparalleled love and strength, who lived with unapologetic confidence and curiosity. She survived wars, refuge, loss, and was the kind of woman who raised her children and grandchildren to love deeply, show up for life, and seek adventure. She used her voice and refused to settle in times when women were seen and not heard. As the dementia progressed, her demeanor changed and she slowly lost her powerhouse personality. I lost the grandma I knew.

The day she cut me off, I was complaining about not being able to afford patio furniture that year. I was feeling sorry for myself, using my time with her to explain how my hopes of outside family dinners, like the ones from my childhood, were ruined for the time being.

This time, instead of listening, she cut me off.

"You are responsible for doing what makes you happy."

Then, back to silence. Chills rushed through my body as I realized my grandma's spirit had briefly come through. It was the first time I remember connecting to it in years, and it's the last time I did before her passing. Her words rang through my head and my heart with the truth. I was playing the victim, and we both knew it. Though she wouldn't remember that moment, I would remember it forever. It felt as though her spirit had woken up and spoken the truth so that I would awaken, too.

I did. I woke up to the fact that I was allowing myself to wallow in circumstances, instead of taking charge and believing in what I could create. The table was a ridiculous manifestation of that, but her words began picking apart my entire life. I started taking an honest look at the things that dragged me down and realized I was allowing myself to play the victim in several areas of life. I started to notice all the places where I felt disempowered, where I shifted blame, or where I told myself stories that my circumstance was what separated me from what I desired. I saw where I had completely opted out of taking responsibility for what I had created in my life.

I had taken the easy way out. The grandma I grew up with was not about to let that happen.

When you wake up to who you are and the possibility of what you can choose to become, you get to live a deeply fulfilling and inspired life, a life that excites and propels you. In that moment, I remembered that I came from a line of women that never settled, and a line of awakened women who saw possibility where others saw dead ends. To claim that I was not made of the same was stifling the fire that was inherent in me. I remembered who I was and that I was in charge of my joy.

My grandmother woke me up, and now I am calling you to wake up, too.

Whether you come from a strong line of women or you are the first one, the message is the same, *"You are responsible for doing what makes you happy. This is your life, and only you can live it well."*

My grandmother's advice has propelled me forward in my self-discovery journey and shone a light on all the places where I needed to heal myself. I discovered many parts of me that needed healing. I began to see where I had completely lost sight of who I was or what I wanted. That realization was deflating. Self-awareness didn't give me the immediate relief or tools to cope, so I felt stuck with an unflattering reflection of myself in many ways. While I made strides in discovering some of my needs and goals, life went on and threw me some curveballs.

Moment 2: The moment I had to step up and lead.

In the moment when I realized that I would bring a child into this world, everything changed. It wasn't unwelcome, just unexpected. I had a profound realization that my life was no longer my own, but that it would be the instrument through which I teach my children the possibility for their lives. My grandmother could never have told me to do what makes me happy if she did not live her life in that way. As a teacher, I also witnessed that children do not do what their parents tell them to do, but embody who their parents are and believe them to be. In my students' words, I heard their parents; for better or worse.

I can't even tell you how many times I've not done something because it needed to be done for myself. When I pursue something outside of my comfort zone for myself, shame, fear, and limiting beliefs take hold more frequently. This is why, even after realizing I needed to take responsibility in my life, heal traumas, and find my passion - I found myself still stuck in habits or experiences that did not serve me. Realizing I wouldn't be able to show my daughter how to live, love, and show up in the world confidently if I wasn't doing it myself fueled my inner flame. I wanted to be better so that she could see and be better, too.

The truth is, living a vibrant and purposeful life may require you to do things you never thought you could do. You may have to end relationships, get out of your comfort zone, suck at something new, upset others, or even restructure the way you live your life. When done in the name of transformation, all of these things can be meaningful but they can also be experiences that have you questioning whether or not you are cut out for the life you desire. Your reason why is the commitment that keeps you going. It's the reason you will show up and step up to be the best version of yourself in life, love, and business.

Motherhood showed me that I was unwilling to compromise when it came to showing my children love, possibility, and purpose. Some days, you may show up to your calling with confidence. Other days, you may feel hopeless or like it's time to give in. It's okay to be scared or discouraged, but remembering your "why" reminds you that this life is worth living and loving anyways.

Moment 3: The moment I choose faith over fear.

Sometimes you are given moments that require you to choose faith or fear. This was one of those moments. Our family had just returned from vacation, and it felt like we were living our best lives. I was feeling confident in my purpose and igniting my passions in business and life. Our family was growing in love and we had welcomed our new baby boy into the world. Then, the next curveball hit.

My mom called me and said she was going in for emergency surgery to get her appendix removed. While alarming, I wished her luck and felt confident that this would be a relatively routine procedure. A couple of days passed and I was none the wiser-- until I was. Apparently, my mom's appendix hadn't been the issue, but rather a tumor was discovered. She didn't tell me about the tumor right away because they had removed what they saw in surgery and she didn't want me to be scared before there was a reason to be. She would be later diagnosed with stage 3 colon cancer at the age of fifty-four.

As I got off the phone, it still didn't feel quite real. Suddenly, everything that my mother was to me flooded my mind and heart. My mother had been an incredible mother who stepped up for me, encouraged me, loved me, and paved the way for me. She had always been my biggest supporter and number one fan. A world without her in it seemed almost unimaginable. I broke down in tears and I was truly afraid of what this meant for all of us. I worried for my mom and my family. If this whole thing went south, my children would be robbed of knowing her and her awesome love.

This terrible moment brought what truly mattered front and center. I realized that most of my daily thoughts and efforts were spent outside of what I truly valued. I'd been confused in thinking that the MORE I achieved or did, the more it mattered. Instead, I saw that what mattered to me most were the relationships and moments with the people I love. Without that love and those people, I suddenly understood that everything I would pursue or create in life would be meaningless. As I cried, I wanted to take back the times that I'd wasted not appreciating my mom. I didn't know what the future held but I was reminded that the ones I love weren't promised to be there.

Through the many months of tests, months of chemo, and days of uncertainty something else became wildly clear to me. I would have to choose between fear and faith. Fear would cripple me. I knew that this time, my mother needed to focus her strength on her healing and my children needed me to continue to lead and pave the way for them. If I folded to fear I would be unable to be strong for any of them. So, with conviction in my heart, I prayed like my life and hers depended on it. I prayed for peace, for healing, for more moments with her, and for light in the darkness. When everything is uncertain, everything that is important becomes clear. Through surrender, I found my peace and courage.

I am blessed to say that my mom is now cancer free and healthy. Life's blessings get a whole lot sweeter when you understand just how blessed you are. When you realize what matters to you, use it as your foundation and build from there. In the moments that make up your life, you will have ones that knock you down, challenge your beliefs, and overwhelm you with sadness and fear. I encourage you to be the kind of woman who faces fear, chooses faith, and has the courage and sense to build a life around what you value and love.

Moment 4: The moment I remembered complacency wasn't enough.

This one was different.

We were friends, we had gone on trips together, and he had held my children. Jake was intertwined in my husband's childhood memories and many of my own.

I picked up the phone to hear my husband say, *"Jake died."* My heart broke for my husband and friends. I couldn't believe it. Jake, the larger than life adventure seeker, dubbed "Superman" by so many who knew him, died of a heart attack playing basketball at thirty-four.

This one was different. A difficult reminder that death has no preference in age, athletic ability, group, or goodness. It was too much of a reminder that if this could happen to Jake, it could happen to anyone.

I reflected on the night we all last saw Jake, and to be honest, I couldn't think of a better memory to be left with. That night created some sense of peace in my heart.

The last night I saw Jake, a friend had a party and the house was filled to the brim with so many of the people that Jake and my husband loved. Jake and my husband grew up like brothers and have a tight-knit group of friends that we call family today. Over the years they became my people, too.

In recent years, Jake had slowly faded from coming to the group gatherings. Even with the realization that we were all getting busier, I knew my husband felt saddened by this and often wondered if they would ever be close again. We hadn't seen Jake in months and when he walked into the party, he immediately lit up the room.

While we mingled, I overheard my husband and Jake reiterating to one another how much they truly loved each other despite the new dynamic in life and friendship. My husband held onto this moment over and over again after Jake's passing with such gratitude. As my husband broke down about Jake, that moment served as a light in a terribly dark experience.

Later on, at the party, I found myself talking to Jake and a few friends. We were talking about split families and I'd said I hoped for others what I had with my son's mom, Kayla. Kayla was a long-time friend of Jake's and best friends with Jake's wife. I mentioned that I was extremely grateful for how Kayla had opened up to me with kindness and graciously supported me in loving our son. Jake interrupted me, *"Chloe, it's because of the person that you are. Because of the way you love him, she is grateful, too."* At that moment, I felt he had shone a light on the goodness inside of me. Goodness that I often forgot to celebrate or even acknowledge. Him seeing me in that light helped me honor that part of me. That moment reminded me that I have goodness inside of me that can't always be measured, yet when shared, is goodness and love nonetheless. This moment became a deeply meaningful memory since he's been gone.

"If you take care of the moments, the years will take care of themselves" – Maria Edgeworth

Jake gifted me with a renewed understanding that one moment can create a ripple. Even more importantly, that our time is a gift for us and when spent in love, a gift to others.

Jake lived life in a way that made you seek freedom, adventure, and truth. If someone that good had something so good to say about the love I had to give, I owed it to myself and to him to share it with the world.

Again, I faced the responsibility to look at the life I was living and ask myself, "How do I live with PURPOSE? RIGHT NOW?"

I was ready to make peace with my past, commit to my future, and promise to step up in my life. Now, not later - because later could be taken away at any moment.

Now, as I get ready to submit this chapter, I know it was because of these moments. Since that time, I have looked fear in the face, written off complacency, and continue to live in pursuit of what lights me up. I'm living out my dreams, and I feel ALIVE.

Whenever you forget just how brave, strong, smart, and loved you are, turn to the moments that help you remember. If you get weary, learn to rest, not to quit. It is your responsibility to do what makes you happy. This is your life, and only you can live it well. When you decide to step up to the moments in your life as the person you desire to be, in a way that feels empowered and fulfilling, in the WAY you wish- that's what I call LIVING.

You may not be perfect, but you are worthy and capable of creating beautiful moments in your life regardless of where you find yourself. Those beautiful moments turn into years, and you will see that you have always been worthy and capable of creating a beautiful life.

If you feel afraid, remember that the moments that you choose to live and love, while yours, may not be yours alone. When your life is over, others will be left with your story and legacy. The moments you find strength, love, connection, and passion in life just might be the moments that others cling to when they need it most. Let this chapter be a reminder to you that in each moment, you are writing your story and that you have a ripple effect.

How will you make the most of each moment in this precious and beautiful life?

What is the ripple you leave behind?

ABOUT CHLOE EVANS

Chloe Evans is a professional educator, coach, creative entrepreneur, and author. Her work as an Intuitive Life Coach teaches women to use their inner tools and guidance to discover their authentic voice, claim their birthright of living their soul's purpose, and attract the experiences they desire.

With over ten years of diving into the principles of manifestation, her vision is to help people discover the clarity, confidence and connection they need to build a life they're wildly obsessed with. She knows that when we feel good, we do good, and when we do better, our children see better. It is this vision of creating a beautiful world of possibility and inspiration for our children that fuels her to cultivate a community of empowered women.

The backbone of her offerings are to inspire connection, creativity, clarity and growth while also inspiring others to connect with their true desires and use that as a foundation to manifest a beautiful life with intention.

When Chloe's not in the classroom, coaching, speaking, or doing workshops, she is most likely playing with her children, diving into her newest design project, or listening to a podcast. Chloe likes to keep it real, loves landscape photography, and almost never wears matching socks (unless she steals them from her husband). She's a lifelong learner with a creative flame and enjoys her beautiful life in Reno, Nevada with her husband and three children. She is available for coaching, speaking engagements, and workshops on a variety of topics including intuition, manifestation, values-based living, and self-love.

Website: www.ChloeAnneEvans.com

Instagram:@lovelightandlifeinspired

Email: missescevans@gmail.com

Facebook Group: Love, Light & Life Inspired

Perfectly Imperfect by Design

Alicia Leigh

I STARED AT MY NEW ARRANGEMENT WITH PRIDE AS THE door opened behind me. My mom peeked her head in wondering, but probably knowing what the commotion was in here. A smile spread across her face, *"Oh honey, I like it this way!"* My expression grew bigger as I turned back to my room with pride. *"I just have no idea how you move this tiny room into so many interesting configurations,"* she chimed as she rubbed my back. This was the third time this month I had rearranged my furniture, but this time, it was perfect… until next week.

My mom was always really good at acknowledging my quirks, both the ones she admired and the ones that utterly baffled her. Things like, *"You're so funny, kiddo!"* to *"I just don't know where you come up with this stuff"* to *"You have to learn not to be so sensitive"* all the way over to *"You are too analytical, Alicia, just let it go."* And I believed it all, the entire spectrum. I don't blame her, though; hell, even I've always been pretty stunned and quite fascinated with myself at times. Some might call it self-centered or egotistical, but I call it introspective and inquisitive. I'm in my own head a lot. I've always wondered why the hell I am the way I am, or why I do the things I do; beyond the fact that I am quite literally an even split of my mom and my biological father. I got a mix of each, so I can actually see where I came from, and yet still... I am perplexed.

Even at a young age, people would say that I was wise beyond my years, that I had an opinion and a word of advice that was on point and usually quite necessary. They were right. I was a wise old owl as I learned, analyzed, and then felt compelled to teach others about rocks, chemistry, human relationships, calligraphy, gymnastics, and well... you name it. If I was curious about it, I dove headfirst into it; for a few months, at least.

In fourth grade, I made friends with a girl (we shall call her Samantha for privacy's sake) and she was an old soul like me. She was the first person I had met who just seemed to think a bit outside the box, or maybe outside the galaxy. We built fairy gardens, talked to ghosts, watched for aliens in the sky, went on adventures, and read each other's astrology charts. People thought she was weird, and maybe she was, but she was also my best friend until I moved away.

I remember arriving at a new school on the first day of seventh grade; it was a crucial time in my life and I knew I wanted to find another Samantha. So, I was determined to make my weird known. I got the chance pretty early on as I caught our science teacher making a joke about how we would have one more second to get to class from now on because they (the scientists who control time, apparently) added ONE second to the year. So, excited about this idea, I raised my hand. Having just started learning a bit about geometry in one of my father's books and from all of my time spent looking at the sky, I explained that it was because the universe was expanding; thus, the circumference was larger and our travel around the sun would be longer. That teacher praised me for my knowledge and put my name on the board for his science club potential member.

I left class feeling pretty damn proud of myself for knowing such an adult concept and really sure that I was going to meet another Samantha this way. That pride and assuredness was suddenly halted by the comments that came thereafter. A group of students had congregated outside the classroom to remind me of my thick glasses, to comment on my short hair, to call me weird-o (which I didn't mind), nerd (not really), then the real stinger "too smart" (um, okay) and then to trip me, causing me to fall down and rip my new jeans.

Now, this was a pivotal moment for me. I knew that I wasn't smart in everything. I was horrible at math, bad at history, and geography completely evaded me while continually providing me the B's and C's that made my mom shrug. I pretty rocked in gym, got in trouble continually in study hall, and loved science, but still struggled to get A's. I was pretty unexceptional in most of my classes, but in this moment, I realized that being exceptional in any moment was a bad thing. Maybe weird wasn't the route to take in this school. Maybe there wasn't a Samantha here. This was the moment that I decided to keep my mouth shut and to blend in, and I did for a long time. That's how I made friends and how I found my clique: I decided to just learn to fit in, and I found a group that would accept this version of me.

I remember feeling very overwhelmed in school despite my curiosity and my newfound ability to fit in. I liked the idea of learning, but not the crap they wanted to teach me. Nope. I wanted hands on, structured, step-by-step learning. Needless to say, I wasn't the best student. I still got my range of A's, B's, and C's. I was perfectly content with my grades mainly because I did very little work to maintain that level of educational homeostasis. The world outside the classroom: that was my playground for learning.

I hit high school feeling completely underprepared and even more underwhelmed. I mean, when did this school thing end? I constantly felt like I was ready for real life to begin. This concept of school was taking up too much of my time when I could be doing much more productive things…like figure out who I was and what I wanted to do without being told what to do. I didn't like it. I wasn't good at it. It was entrapment, I tell you!

At this time in any young person's life, there are a lot of questions. The ones that confused me the most were the ones like, *"What do you want to do when you grow up?"* and *"What college do you plan to attend?"* and *"What sport do you want to do next season?"* People started to recognize that I wasn't one to stick with the same thing for long, so WHY then did they actually think I would have an answer for them now? I mean, those are all months and years away, so why ask when I'm just going to change my mind, right?

But, I was supposed to know. Clearly. This was the time in my life when my peers started knowing. Cate wanted to play the violin and go to a liberal arts college to study music. Sally wanted to pursue a career on Broadway. Nick wanted to become a doctor, so he had his AP classes lined up through senior year. Amanda was really good at basketball, so she knew she wanted to start by sophomore year and win a state title before she graduated. People were starting to pick their colleges. People had been playing their sport or their instrument for ten years at this point. But not me, oh no, not me.

I had no idea what I wanted to do. I had about twenty-five colleges on my list… all for very different reasons. I left the flute behind the third week of playing it, but I did teach myself the keyboard and mastered two songs before I got bored. I had just quit the ski team in my first season to try out for cheerleading. I got hurt doing gymnastics. Track was really starting to become a snooze fest. I did do international club for two years, which was quite the feat, but I stayed with it mainly because they had really good food at all of the meetings. I was learning a lot across all categories, but I started to notice that I wasn't "sure" about anything, and it seemed that everyone else was.

This was most apparent to me when I sat down with my high school counselor halfway through the first semester of my junior year. She pulled out a piece of paper that appeared to be a checklist and began asking a series of questions that I quickly noted were about my future plans for college. Questions like, *"When are you scheduled to take the SAT?"* and *"What is the math class you want to take your senior year?"* and *"Have you started college applications for early decision yet?"* My head began to spin with each answer ending in, *"No, I don't know"* or *"What, already?"*

It was then that I realized: I was behind. My counselor saw it, too. She put her pen down gently and picked her head up from the downward gaze she had maintained up to this point. Looking me square in the eyes she said, *"Alicia, I have been with you since middle school. I have seen your* intelligence, your personality, your magnetism, and your ability to do anything you want to do. But I'm also watching you also fall short of your potential. You need to pick something, pick one thing; one field of study, one school, one sport even and choose it quickly so you can focus on it. Without this focus, you will never live up to your fullest potential." My heart sank.

You see, I'm a people pleaser. Yep, in every way, all I want to do is to please those around me by proving how amazing I am at x, y, and z. I blame it on the fact that my parents separated when I was very young; I had a tumultuous childhood with one side full of restriction and judgement while the other side had instability and insecurity. All of that was mixed with abuse and their abilities to get married and divorced a total of seven times. I was pretty sure that everyone leaves and that I wasn't good enough to make people stick around or love me in the ways I thought might be most healthy. Now, I know with every fiber of my being that I love these two people who created me dearly, they did the very best they could, they raised me based on what they knew, learned, and what was passed down to them. My mother is one of the most caring and generous humans you will ever meet, and boy does she love me; that's never been the question. My biological father is one of the smartest men I've ever met, he is fiscally responsible, and a dependable rock of structure. I was lucky to have a final step-father who, though he missed my most malleable years, stepped up to the plate and became one of the most honorable men that I would later call Dad. They're all good people, they're all human in their own right, but I definitely learned that if I acted a certain way or became a certain person, I would either make them proud or cause more turmoil than they could handle.

So, I lived my life up to this point pretty low-key, causing just a bit of trouble, but not too much. I was smart in certain areas but didn't show it off. I was athletic all around but didn't brag about anything I achieved. I was in a lot of groups but didn't try to really stick with one too hard. I switched sports and interests when I felt it was time. I didn't rock any boats. I didn't try to stand out or to attempt extraordinary and if or when I did, I would quietly remind myself of the consequences. Inside I was shrinking, but externally, I seemed to be doing okay. I was skimming by and things were good.

It wasn't until adulthood that I realized "skimming and getting by" weren't exactly the pillars for an extraordinary life. I felt a pull towards something more. So, as I earned my three national titles and four degrees, while I worked my one million jobs, while I hit multiple six figures in the multiple companies that I built, while getting my pro cards in two bodybuilding categories, and while dating every type of person in an attempt to figure out who I was meant to be and who I was meant to be with... the questions began again.

They started with the family asking, *"When are you going to settle down?"* Friends then started asking, *"Alicia, when are you going to pick something?"* to comments like *"You're too ambitious"* or *"You're a lot to handle"* and *"You're too…analytical, emotional, needy, busy, scattered, unfocused" and the one that hurt me the most,* "You will have to settle at some point." I started to question it all and I started to create the answers that made others happy.

I started to shrink my dreams, and even worse, when I did show up for them again I did them from a place of deep-rooted fear. I started hating myself for wanting more. I found myself jealous of others for having more. I was becoming fearful of receiving. I hit a state of depression that I wouldn't wish on anyone. I found myself actually believing that death would be easier than this less of a life I was being forced to live.

It was in those moments that my sense of logic was exhausted, my "intelligence" diminished just enough that I let a bit of magic seep in. I was perusing the internet for my next "solution" when I came across a post that hit me hard. I don't remember the exact words today, but paraphrased it read something like this, *"Life doesn't have to be this hard, you are making it harder because you're fighting the innate principles of who you are. DM for a human design reading."* I immediately messaged her.

We did a human design reading the very next week, and that was the week that it all changed for me. I remembered that inner child that rearranged her furniture and picked up hobbies that spurred her interest, back to the days when life and learning got to be fun and experimental without judgement or ridicule. I got to be a more innate version of myself again, one who tries it all while learning through hands-on play and active participation in her own life.

You see, I am a 3/5 emotional manifestor in human design. I was always meant to do, see, try, create; and to do all that without reason or cause. It's not erratic, it's manifesting. It's my human design. I was never meant to "niche down" or to "find my thing." I was always meant to learn through trial and error so that I could help those who don't learn this way to avoid my mistakes altogether.

To say that call changed my very existence is an understatement. It was during that call that I found an inner acceptance that I had never seen or heard before. The statements said to me my whole life of, *"You're too emotional, too analytical, too hard to get to know, too hard to connect with, too cold, too scattered and flighty, and also basically not enough,"* were summed up in sixty minutes and one phrase: *"This is how you were designed."* The tears began to flow, but this time with an absolute freedom, release, and an overarching understanding of myself, my innate being, and the person I was born to be. My human design was always enough and never too much - all at the same time.. My human design is strong and powerful. My human design is me, the me that I was born to be who is multi-passionate, overtly forthright in my doing and achieving, and serves women who are, too. My human design gives me the acceptance of me that I wish to pass on to others who have struggled with being them.

My design is unique to me.

Your design is unique to you.

So, the "too much" or "too little" that you are for anyone other than you is just too darn bad for them. Shrinking to fit the "right amount" of anything serves no one. YOU are beautifully designed as just enough of all of the good stuff the universe had to offer when you were created. YOU are magic, always.

ABOUT ALICIA LEIGH

Alicia Leigh was born in Maine where she lived until age nineteen. After graduating high school in Farmington, Maine she moved to Kentucky where she completed all four of her degrees including two Bachelor's and two Associate's degrees while cheerleading and competing nationally to win three national co-ed titles and two 4th place partner stunt finishes.

After leaving the world of competitive cheerleading and chasing college degrees, she went on to take the fitness world by storm, winning 6 of the 10 competitions she competed in, and earning her pro cards in two categories in 2015. During her time in the fitness world, Alicia built a successful competition suit design company, which she sold the rights to in 2010. With a newfound openness in her normally jam-packed schedule, she moved on to create a six figure personal training and online coaching business, as well as a multiple six figure network marketing company with team members spanning across all 50 states and 5 countries, earning her top <1% of the company in earnings.

Desiring to make use of her degrees, Alicia saw an opening in the cardiovascular perfusion field and decided to contract her services for a company at a local hospital. Realizing how much downtime she had at this position between patients, she created a healthcare contract company using all of her certifications to contract calorimetry, ECMO management, as well as home health respiratory services to create her third six figure endeavor.

Having realized her aptitude toward building businesses, she began a coaching business in 2018 to help others do the same. She now utilizes her knowledge of human design to help women build lives and businesses that are authentically aligned and energetically profitable through her company "ByDesign" while also utilizing her creative skills to build a business as a permanent makeup artist rightfully called "BeautifullyDesigningYou".

To connect with Alicia:

Alicia@TheHumanDesignHub.com for business by design coaching

Or

Alicia@BeautifullyDesigningYou.com for beautifully
designed lashes, brows, lips and skin

Facebook:
https://www.facebook.com/TheHumanDesignHub

Instagram:
https://www.instagram.com/AliciaLeigh_ThatsMe

Website:
www.YouAreBeautifullyDesigned.com or
www.TheHumanDesignHub.com

Lenses of Love

Blair Hayse

IT TOOK ME A LONG TIME TO BE ABLE TO FACE MY INNER demons. The one where I had no idea what I believed and where I stood on many universal principles. I grew up in a strict fundamental religious home. One where beliefs were not allowed to be questioned. My naturally curious mind could not help but question them internally. I had a stubborn mind and a quick tongue, so I am pretty sure I tested my parent's patience along the way. I never wanted anything fed to me as to what I needed to believe. I wanted to figure it out on my own and decide for myself not only WHAT I believed, but WHY I believed it. Only then would I feel concrete in my belief system. I spent much of my childhood and teenage years told what to believe and every ounce of my being rebelled inside. Not particularly because the beliefs were wrong (I choose to believe that everyone has their own version of truth), but because I was told to believe them.

Somewhere in my teenage years, one of the very beings who was a crux in telling me what to believe, also gave me the answers to my need to seek deeper reasons in why I believed it. She didn't know it at the time and she might even turn over in her grave as I type this out, but she gave me the keys to send me to freedom, even all those years ago. She handed me an old Catholic bible that was sitting on her shelf. I took it and I dove into it. I read up on why it was different from the bible I was taught from every day in my home. I wanted to know the difference. I wanted to know why parts were taken away. I wanted to know more and more. I needed answers. I didn't want to just believe a book on the shelf because I was told to believe it. I wanted to believe it because I knew I should.

When I left home at eighteen, things were not easy for me. My parents and I quit talking. I was bitter at them and I am pretty sure they chalked me up as a failed child or prodigal daughter. Over the next three years of our strained, non-existent relationship I struggled to even believe there was a higher power. I tried to attend church and many times walked out in the middle of the service. I didn't want to hear any of the rubbish about unconditional love when I didn't see it present in my life. I would go from begging if there was a higher presence to please give me answers to not believing there was anyone to even talk to that cared up there. I attended every service there was out there. If you have a question about a religion, I bet I could answer it. I went to Baptist, non-denominational,

Methodist, Presbyterian, Catholic, Lutheran, and even Unitarian. There was one point I attended a Jewish temple, Islamic Mosque and pagan church. I explored all of it. I wanted to know why every one of them believed what they did. I never took what they gave me as truth, but I asked questions and really listened when they explained their beliefs. I dove deep into it all. Luckily, my parents had given me a bible that was in Greek and Hebrew. I went into the original language and researched how it had been translated to English. Did it mean the same thing? Did it say the same thing? Had it been lost in translation? I left no stone unturned.

In all of my research, I found that some religious leaders were absolutely sure that their path was the ONLY path. They would be the first to tell me that I needed to join their community and adapt to their beliefs. Many felt threatened if I questioned them to explain to me why they believed what they taught and to show me where they found evidence it should be that way. However, there was one class I took that I never felt that way. The leader let me ask as many questions as I wanted. He encouraged it. He knew I was asking out of pure curiosity of what I wanted to know. He knew I was seeking the answers deep within to find my own beliefs. He answered every question with patience. Never did he tell me that what he was telling me was the only way. He never once told me I HAD to believe what he was saying. We had some really deep conversations around the translations and the other languages involved. I dug deep into Latin to understand the roots of words. Everything piqued my interest to dig deeper. I didn't want to just be out here not knowing what to believe. I didn't want to feel lost and as if I had no beliefs. I just needed to find out WHAT I believed, WHY I believed it and HOW I chose to practice what I believe. When the end of that class came he invited the members to continue the process of steps to join the church. I went to him and was honest with him. I told him I believed most of what he had said. For the first time, I actually saw how rooted what he told me was in the original language and in the history of the "church" if one must call it that. It was the first place I felt peace. I felt like I belonged in my soul. I could walk in and immediately have answers in my inner being. He looked me in the eye and asked me three very targeted "do you believe" questions. To each I said yes. "That is all it takes," he said, "the rest is really up to you to determine what it means to you. You believe the basic core truths and that is all I care about. We all might have different paths to get there." I was surprised. Mainly because I could have never imagined hearing that from some of the other leaders I had come in contact with. I proceeded to change my religion and the place I would call my community of belief.

In the years that followed, I continued to dig even deeper. Anytime I ran across something I did not understand or that I wondered if I was wrong to believe

I went to this leader. I sat in his office many days and learned from him. He had an in-depth cultural knowledge and he understood my need for deeper answers. He didn't believe in cookie cutter beliefs. Like me, he believed that every person had their own interpretation based on what was given to them by the divine inspiration from above. His gracious nature and loving approach to religion in general is what brought me back to my roots. He helped me untangle all that I had been taught. Helped me decide what internally I believed based on what I knew as my truth. He helped me see things from a higher perspective. He taught me the basics of meditation and looking within. To not only call out to the Universe, but listen as it answered.

I walked my own path of truth. I leaned into what it was that I believed to be true and knew exactly why I believed it. I became unwavering in what I chose to do with my life. I became sure of why I chose to do the things I did. I found an internal compass and peace I had never known in my life. When I made bad choices, I could get back on track easily without beating myself up or waiting for some drastic condemnation to sweep me up. I quit living in FEAR and chose to live in true FAITH. The best part is I learned it is never a one stop process. Faith is continually evolving. Our beliefs are continually growing. Things that we once saw one way, we can see differently when we are in a different place of growth later. It all comes to us if we get quiet and listen to what our internal compass is telling us.

There were things that happened in my earlier life that I am choosing to not put in this book chapter. Mainly, because they were demons I had to face internally. While I blamed my parents for the demons, in all honesty, it was part of my path. Without them, I would have never learned to dig deeper into my heart. I am grateful for all of it. Even after finding my peace within, I struggled to forgive my parents. We started talking shortly after that and tried to rebuild our relationship. I still held a lot of bitterness towards them. One day, my dad took me for a drive and he asked me, "What was one thing I did that made you so angry with me and hurt you the most?" I answered honestly. I do not think what I told him was what he expected to hear. To him I am sure he thought that incident was trivial, but to me it created a hatred in my heart towards him. He looked at me in shock and apologized with tears in his eyes. One thing I can safely say is my dad will always admit when he is wrong. It is something I have admired of him and to this day, and try to practice it with my own children. As I watched the tears stream down his face, I realized something I had not realized before. My dad did not do those things to hurt me. He honestly thought at the time what he was doing was best for me. He was trying to make sure I was raised well. My dad never physically hurt me or abused me growing up. Looking back, he gave me a warm home, I never worried about food, he took us on trips as a family and showed me true love. He never meant harm in what he chose as rules for the home. For the first time, it was as if I saw my dad in the eyes of love. A love that realized he loved me and all he did was out of love.

In that moment of realization, I loved my dad deeper than I had in years. As I became a parent I understood him on a level I never did before. Did I attend many years of therapy for the beliefs I had adapted in childhood and patterns I wanted to break? Yes. Will my kids probably do the same? Probably. I am not perfect. One thing I can assure them is that I have tried to break some of the generational patterns and cycles for them. I hope that they recognize patterns I did not and they choose to break those. That would thrill my heart because it shows me that they are growing even more than me and to create an even better life for those after me. When I have conversations with my children now, I see where they are in such a place of growth that I never was at their age. I know they are destined to achieve even higher levels of truth in their quest of life.

So many people have asked me how I healed. The truth is, I saw it from the eyes of love. I saw it as they did the best they could and that is good enough for me. Both my parents had generational patterns they chose to break as well. My dad chose to break the generational pattern of alcoholism that he grew up in. My mother works hard daily to break a generational pattern of negative talk and beliefs that was handed down to her. I see things now from a higher level. I see two people who had their own patterns to break. That, my friends, is how I healed. Love. I hope my children see me through those same lenses when they have to break patterns I did when I was still learning.

I encourage my children to reach for their healing inside. Knowing what they believe and why they choose to believe it. I want them to know that just because I believe something doesn't mean that is what they must believe. It is up to them to find their truth. I want them to know I support them no matter what that inner truth is for them. I want them to be happy, feel loved and to be a conduit for their own healing. I want them to know that so much can be seen when you choose to look through the lenses of love. It brings a whole new perspective to life and to others. The judgements fall away and in its place is an inner peace.

I now love my parents on a whole new level and have seen them grow in the years. They are human, of course they make mistakes, but I see it differently now. I still go to them for advice, support and trust them immensely. The greatest gift of healing you can give yourself is to look at what has hurt you or who has hurt you with the eyes of love. Choose to see it from a higher place. In this, you give yourself forgiveness. You give others forgiveness. You find peace and you find healing. You allow yourself to be you and to stand in your truth. You don't feel the need to force your truth on others. You don't feel the need to always be heard. Love changes all. It certainly can change you, your healing and your peace. It is magical the transformation it can create.

Until next time, look through the lenses of love.

You are Magic!

ABOUT BLAIR HAYSE

Blair was born and raised in Tupelo, Mississippi. After graduating high school in 1999 she lived in Birmingham and Florence, Alabama before moving back to Itawamba County, Mississippi in 2008. She is an avid yoga lover, free spirit, shopping addict and mom to three beautiful children Parker, Millie and Jackson. She is currently residing in Northeast Mississippi and enjoys traveling in her spare time.

Blair has a 19-year background in Corporate America where she worked with billion-dollar companies such has Hilton, Marriott, IHG, Starwood and others. She was called in to create a massive profit in a business so that the company could flip the business or make an investment.

She specialized in working with business investments that had gone bad so that a quick profit could be achieved.

Some of her projects included businesses that had been costing the company money for five years straight and she brought them to a massive profit level in just six months. This became her signature method of seven figures in six months that she used over and over.

Blair created a legacy in the corporate world where she was sought out for her expertise. The corporate life while exciting and well-paying was exhausting to the single mom of two kids. Blair brought her skills to the online world where she began to help online businesses create a massive flow of profit in a short amount of time. This allowed her the freedom to enjoy her life, travel more and give time to her family.

Blair recently took her interests to her own passion since childhood...writing. She owns Blair Hayse Publishing which offers all-inclusive services to authors to publish their works and create best-selling authors. She offers collaboration books to new authors to build them their own platform. Just this year alone she has helped 60 women become best-selling authors. She writes for Thrive Global and Elephant Journal regularly. You can purchase her books on Amazon under her own author page.

Blair currently is a Visibility Coach, four-time best-selling author and international speaker. She supports her authors in increasing their platforms and using their books as leverage in their business. She also offers free resources and paid programs to those interested in furthering their writing experience to become an author. She hosts a semi-annual conference which usually averages around 400 attendees and offers private coaching to her clients. Recently her company has founded a non-profit sector, RISE Movement, Inc. where they are supporting those who need it most to provide reading and writing opportunities. You can join her FREE Facebook group for some massive value at: Society of Experts.

To connect with Blair:

blairhayse@gmail.com or blairhayseceo@blairhayse.com

Facebook: https://www.facebook.com/blairhayse/

Instagram: https://www.instagram.com/blairhayse/

You Can Go Your Own Way

Stephanie Scimeca

I AM HOLDING A STICK TALLER THAN ME IN THE MIDDLE OF winter. My father, my two sisters and I had just completed a round of sledding and we were now playing in the snow. My dad is filming us with a typical 1980's style, enormous camcorder. I take my stick, use it as a walking pole, and trek up a snow pile. It was a mountain in my eyes at the time. I boast loudly, *"I claim this mountain, in the name of the Earth!"* I guess I was a space cadet. Who can really say?

When I was a child, I dreamed of being an explorer. I dreamed of far off places and animals. I could spend hours upon hours at a time reading *Zoobooks* and playing on my *Encyclopedia Britannica* for fun. Back then, *Encyclopedia Britannica* came on a floppy disc and let you look at pictures of people, places, and things with sound effects. It was incredible.

As I grew older, my interest in adventure grew. Like most others my age I spent a great deal of time playing Oregon Trail, but I also played Amazon Trail. I dreamed of the day that I could float on a canoe down the Amazon River. Zoos, aquariums, climbing trees, catching and rescuing animals were some of my favorite pastimes. In the first grade, I organized a park cleanup for my local park. With script in hand, I nervously walked up to the loud speaker and made an announcement about how the pollution in our park was ruining it and that it was important for us all to do something. I read a modified version of *Moby Dick* at the age of eight because the cover looked like a grand adventure. By the fourth grade, I was reading Jack London's *White Fang* and *Call of the Wild*. I felt so deeply connected to these stories- to being in the great unknown, the wilderness, traveling, and connecting with nature. Fortunately, all of the resources I had at my disposal kept this dream alive within me, even when it was pushed deep inside by societal pressures.

I did all of the right things in school. I was a grade A student throughout my entire academic career. I was part of the Gifted and Talented club in elementary school, took AP classes in my junior and senior years of high school, and maintained a GPA that kept me in the top of my class. I was hard on myself. If I got below a 100% on an exam, I would beat myself up about it more than my parents would. I was told time and time again that school would be the ticket to a full and happy life. That it would provide me with options and "solid job prospects." The older I got, the less keeping up these appearances felt right. I loathed that it was normal to pit students against one another. I slowly started to pull away and disengage. I didn't want to be a part of the rat race. I didn't care if I got into Ivy League schools or not. I just wanted to be happy.

It also didn't help that I didn't know what I wanted to do with myself and my life. Internally, I battled with my own thoughts. *Maybe I'm not good enough to do anything. Why can't I decide on something like everyone else can? Why can't I just figure it out? What's wrong with me?* These thoughts would resurface time and time again.

In my freshman year of college, I was flailing. All of my friends and roommates at school seemed to have a clear direction, a clear purpose. I remember standing in the middle of campus watching students move with such a strong sense of purpose, with such deliberate actions. I felt like a complete outsider, lost in the crowd. I sought out a therapist on campus. I have been in and out of therapy for the majority of my life as I have struggled with depression and anxiety since the age of twelve. At this particular moment in time, the main thing we focused on was becoming comfortable with uncertainty. My therapist gave me the book by Pema Chodron, *Comfortable with Uncertainty: 108 Teachings*. I clung to this for support for a while afterward. I started embracing Buddhist teachings about permanence and I began trying to focus only on the here and now, not being depressed about the past or anxious about the future. Easier said than done, but I revisit these teachings every now and again when I feel myself starting to fall apart.

Still unsure what I should be doing with myself and seeking some sort of lifeline, some direction, I circled back to my childhood dream. One of them, anyway. Since I found out that explorers were pretty much no longer a thing and all of the Earth had been mostly mapped out, I had to fall back on my other love: animals. I decided that I wanted to be a veterinarian. This made my parents quite happy - a doctor in the family, perfect! I found a job working as a veterinary assistant at a local animal hospital. A plan started to come together. While I had been undeclared for my first year or so at school, I decided that it was time to make a commitment to something. My family and others kept asking me, *What are you planning to do with your life? What career do you want? Don't you want stability?* Seemingly, becoming a veterinarian would do all of those things for me and get them off my back.

I applied to a pre-vet program at another university. I was accepted and was excited about this new opportunity laid before me. I would be embarking on a new adventure-leaving the state and going to a new school up in the mountains. The campus was beautiful, and everything felt like it was falling into place. *I have a life plan after all!*

But, life isn't always that easy. It turned out that my family couldn't afford the college tuition, as we only qualified for so much financial aid, so my plan quickly fell apart. *Okay. My plans have totally fallen through. I need to pick myself back up. Clearly being a veterinarian isn't for me. So now what?*

I had another fork in the road ahead of me. I transferred to a local college. I still felt like I needed a clean slate. I no longer felt like I belonged at my current university. Since I had completed all of my required courses, I was now able to choose any courses that I wanted. I took everything that sounded interesting: philosophy, anthropology, sociology, yoga, archaeology, oceanography. I fell in love. Anthropology spoke to my soul in ways that no other courses had ever done before. I connected with them so deeply, on so many levels. Adventure was inherent in the discipline- traveling to new places, meeting new people, learning about new cultures and people. I almost immediately changed majors and pursued anthropology with a sociology minor. A few years later, I graduated.

Life was looking up again. I was living my life on my own terms, becoming more independent and embracing my new prospects. My parents never did understand what I could do with an anthropology degree, but it didn't matter to me. I knew I would figure it out someday.

The deeper I dove into anthropology, the more I loved it. My role model became Lara Croft, the Tomb Raider and video game character. She had everything that I wanted and more: adventure, smarts, strength, and a killer bod. Naturally, I turned to fitness and became a fitness coach while simultaneously pursuing a graduate degree in anthropology.

Even though my days were pretty monotonous in terms of my routine, going to work, going to school, working out, taking care of homework and other tasks at home, I felt that I was on the right path again. One day, I was folding my laundry at my parent's house as I was still living at home at the time. My dad walked into the room and said, *"Look how domestic you are."* My skin crawled. *Domestic?! The absolute last thing I want to be is domestic.* I could vomit at the word. Suddenly, everything was thrown into turmoil within me once more. I was not living up to the idea of what I wanted in my head for myself. I did not want to be *domestic*.

The undertones from my family were growing louder. Through all of my exploration, my trials and tribulations, my experiments with different jobs and majors, my parents wanted a career for me. They wanted me to settle, buy a house, have a family. They wanted me to put down roots. I didn't want anything to do with any of that. Hearing it all gave me the heebie jeebies. I thought about my favorite Disney princess, Pocahontas. I felt her pain when her father wanted her to take the husband of his choosing, who was "steady like the river," when in fact, "the river isn't steady at all." I didn't want to be steady. I wanted to find what's around the riverbend.

I left my job as a veterinary assistant. It took a long time- I was there for eight years and I appreciated the stability and flexibility of that job while everything else in my life seemed to be in turmoil. But, the time had come for me to venture out into the great beyond. I got into the travel business with the hopes of expanding my horizons and increasing my ability to see the world. Unfortunately, this job option didn't last long. Surprisingly, it was an incredibly toxic environment. The rat race reared its ugly head again. As agents, we were expected to sell, sell, sell and earn the highest commissions possible for our office. It was a competition among every office across the country. For a while, it was fun. I even enjoyed the challenge. But when it started taking a toll on my mental health, I knew I had to call it quits. I ended up staying in the travel field but switching companies. With my background, I worked on the back-end of things: finalizing travel documents, dotting i's and crossing t's, making sure that travel visas and passports were up to date and accurate for travel. It was easy, but not challenging. The monotony of the job accompanied a failing relationship and left me to reevaluate my life.

What do I want to do?

I searched the depths of my soul until I found that adventurous child inside of me.

I want to apply to the Peace Corps.

I almost immediately called a recruiter. She told me straight up that I needed to beef up my resume in education. I had some background as a tutor, mentor, etc., but it was not enough for the work I would be doing in the field. After a few days of research, I decided that the best way for me to get education experience was to actually get into education. So, I applied to teaching programs: a mix of traditional programs through schools and "fast-track" programs like Teach for America and the New York City Teaching Fellows (NYCTF). I was accepted into a college education program and the NYCTF.

The New York City Teaching Fellows was one of the most strenuous and draining programs I have ever completed, and that is saying something having already pursued graduate studies. As part of the program, you are thrust into a six-week bootcamp to learn the foundations of teaching while working at summer school. You are also put into a two-year master's degree program along with working full-time as a teacher. I was up at the crack of dawn each day and went to sleep incredibly late each night. I worked harder than I ever had before in my life, but I did it and it felt great. I felt that I had a sense of purpose again. I graduated with a Master's of Science in Education, and I have now been a teacher for five years at a school in the Bronx.

Teaching is impossibly hard on so many levels. It is emotionally, physically, mentally, and spiritually draining. As a teacher, you are expected to wear multiple hats in a single day and switch them from minute to minute. The health, wellness, and education of your students is in your hands. There are millions of miles of red tape in the bureaucracy of it all, and you are fighting systems of oppression from within the system; a cog in an enormous wheel. But you show up day in and day out for your students. Somehow, I excel in this role. I have become a leader of the Special Education department, I supervise multiple people working with our students with disabilities, I help drive our science department to push for inquiry-based learning and expand our curriculums to incorporate real science-based practices in the classroom. It even allows me to travel during my summer vacations. I have been to the Amazon (my childhood dream) because of this job. Still, something within me pulls at me. Something doesn't feel right.

This is the career my parents wanted for me. It's "stable" with benefits and has a retirement plan and a pension. It's socially acceptable. They feel good saying that their daughter is a teacher. It holds some weight in their social circles, albeit not as much as a doctor or lawyer.

But what if I want more? Something different?

This push and pull within me is constant. It has been with me since I was a child, and I do not think it will ever go away. I am not sure I will ever be satisfied staying in a single job or career for the rest of my life. I'm not sure I am someone who can put down roots. Maybe I'm more like an air plant and less like a great oak tree. Maybe I'm more like Pocahontas and Moana and less like Cinderella and Belle. Because I keep asking myself, *"what if?"* and I can't live without knowing the answer.

My journal reads: *The hardest part of all of this is saying, out loud, that I DON'T WANT THIS LIFE.*

So, I'm pursuing yet another graduate degree. This time a Masters in Biology with an emphasis on Conservation. I am working in conjunction with the Wildlife Conservation Society. Next year, I hope to be in Thailand learning about the connections between Buddhism and conservation. Will this be the only thing I ever do again? Maybe, but maybe not. What's next for me? Maybe a PhD. I have always wanted to be called a doctor. But maybe I'll go into business. Maybe I'll start a non-profit. Who knows?

I have had upwards of sixteen different jobs in different fields throughout the course of my life thus far. Some may call me flaky or unstable. I call it learning through experience. I have taken something from each and every single one of those experiences and applied them to the next thing I got myself into. Perhaps I will never be a dedicated expert in any one thing, but I now consider myself a multi-passionate empath. I am interested and I care about so many different things. Moving around allows me to explore each of these passions, and has presented me with incredible and unique challenges.

The back and forth between what I want and what was acceptable for me to want was exhausting. But it was something I knew I would need to navigate to fit into society and not be looked down upon by my family. I have come to accept that I don't want what my family wants for me, and that's okay. I can have any combination of things in my life that I want. I can have a clean apartment and not just be considered some "domestic" woman. *I can be a walking contradiction.* I'm okay with that. Because at the end of the day, I am the one faced with looking at myself in the mirror. I have to follow my own bliss and pursue my own happiness. If this sounds like you, you can have that, too. Despite what your friends, your family, and society tells you, you can find out what's around the riverbend. You can find out how far the water goes. Lastly, in the words of my namesake Stevie Nicks and Fleetwood Mac, "You can go your own way."

Disney's Moana - How Far I'll Go:

"I've been staring at the edge of the water

'Long as I can remember, never really knowing why

I wish I could be the perfect daughter

But I come back to the water, no matter how hard I try

Every turn I take, every trail I track

Every path I make, every road leads back

To the place I know, where I cannot go

Where I long to be

See the line where the sky meets the sea

It calls me

And no one knows, how far it goes

If the wind in my sail on the sea stays behind me

One day I'll know

If I go there's just no telling how far I'll go"

ABOUT STEPHANIE SCIMECA

Stephanie is a born and raised New Yorker originally from Long Island and currently resides in Manhattan. She is an introverted extrovert Sagittarian empath, which says a lot. Stephanie is an adrenaline junkie who is afraid of heights, but forces herself to do all of the things regardless. She is a cat and struggling plant mom. In her spare time, she loves to travel and do literally anything that combines being outdoors and movement including, but not limited to, hiking, biking, kayaking, snorkeling, and skiing. She is always reading at least three books at a time and learning skills like how to play a steel drum or scrimshaw.

Stephanie has had dozens of jobs since she was able to get her working papers at the age of 14. From face painter to movie theater concession staff to veterinary assistant, she considers herself a multipotentialite and pursues everything that draws her heart and soul to it. Stephanie is a life-long learner who has completed multiple degrees, and continues to do so. She has a bachelor's degree in Anthropology with a minor in Sociology, has pursued graduate studies in Anthropology, Special Education, and is currently pursuing another master's degree in Biology, with an emphasis in conservation.

Stephanie is currently a Special Education teacher in New York City. She is an expert in specialized instruction, differentiation, and working with students in creating successful post-secondary goals and plans. Stephanie leads the special education department, supervises Individualized Education Plan (IEP) case managers, and is the Transition Team Leader at her school. She also specializes in diversity and inclusion in an education setting for persons with disabilities and the LGBTQIA+ community. Additionally, she is an environmental educator exploring environmental justice issues impacting BIPOC communities and focusing on incorporating conservation optimism into the classroom as a tool for engaging youth in the conservation field.

LinkedIn:
https://www.linkedin.com/in/stephaniescimeca/

Email:
Stephanie.Scimeca@Gmail.com

Sign Posts of Mint and Rose

~Meeting Ancestry~

Mayuko Fukino

A LONG, DARK-HAIRED LADY IN A FLORAL KIMONO ON A boat in the quiet ocean. A bright, full moon is shining upon her as if the moon is watching over her path. That's how a channeler just described a scene that he received as he is holding both of my hands. I'm completely in awe, because I've never met this channeler in my life and I'm confused how he knows my recurring dream. He opens his eyes and stares into mine. In a hurry, before my time is up, he says, *"You are a powerful healer. You know that, right? Heritage. Return to your heritage. It is extremely important that you return to your heritage."*

I went home and *"return to your heritage"* continued to echo in my head. As the word *"heritage"* echoed in my head, I fell asleep while looking at the full moon through a window. Again, I see the same dream where the moon is brighter than ever. In the dream, the word *"heritage"* is echoing again. Each time I dream this dream, I know exactly where I am. However, when I wake up from the dream, I don't know where it is, but I know that is where I belong and that is what I am supposed to be doing.

While I still don't know what *"returning to heritage"* is supposed to mean, a few days after the session with the channeler, I have an astrology reading by Gregory Paul Martin. His profound and deep voice echoed into my ears saying, *"You must know you are a psychic. You are a powerful healer, but not everyone is going to come to you because you are an esoteric healer."*

Again, *"return to your heritage"* echoes in my head. From yet another reader, I'm told that I'm a healer. I'm not sure what I'm supposed to do to claim myself as a healer. Then, I hear the word *"heritage"* again.

I was born and raised in Japan between the ages of six and sixteen years old. By this time, I'm forty-nine years old. I'm living in the United States, have four children, and am remarried. Returning to my heritage seems far away and feels too much financially and mentally, but the words *"return to your heritage"* keep echoing in my head.

When I hear the same word over and over again, I have learned to ask my Spirit Guides to show me the answer in my dreams. For some reason, I am almost scared to ask what the meaning of *"returning to heritage"* means.

In the dream, I hear again, *"Return. You will know."*

My Spirit Guides are patient. It's probably because they know I'm stubborn. When I decide to surrender and drop my guard, my father happens to call me to invite me, all of my children, and my husband to Japan. My finances are all taken care of. It's as if someone wants me to be there.

I'm excited, but at the same time I'm scared. One of my spiritual and psychic friends tells me that it will be a *"one-of-a-kind spiritual journey."* I feel the butterflies fluttering in my stomach as if I'm meeting the love of my life. My friend tells me again, *"Returning to your heritage is the ultimate spiritual journey that you don't forget."*

I feel it as if I'm already there, but I don't know what is happening or what I'm supposed to do. Again, I hear my Spirit Guides whispering, *"You will know. Trust. Return to your heritage."*

I have taken the same trip to Tokyo to visit my family so many times before, but on this day of flying I felt excitement and sleepiness (resulted from not being able to sleep the night before like a hyper-excited kid.) *"Why am I feeling this way? Is it because I'm going on my 'spiritual journey'?"*

While I'm in the sky for ten hours, I have the recurring dream…being in the kimono, on the bamboo boat in the ocean, and under the bright, full moon. I ask, *"What am I supposed to know? What am I supposed to do? Where am I supposed to go?"* Again, I hear, *"Return to your heritage. Trust. You will know."*

I arrived in Tokyo with one of my daughters. I think my father has some kind of clue to what I'm supposed to know, to what I'm supposed to do, and where I'm supposed to go, but I find out he doesn't even have any set plans on where he is going to take us.

All I can think of is to entertain my daughter until my other daughters and my husband unite with us. Then I receive a call from a new friend, Mr. Kawakami (I only know him from email). He creates titanium sound bowls that are very similar to the sound I keep hearing in the recurring dream and I had been wanting to tangibly play them.

I asked my Spirit Guides, *"Here is my budget. Is it for me and my daughters to go?"* I hear again *"Trust. Return to your heritage."* I'm dying to try the sound bowls and hear them in person, but I have never met him and there is no family there.

I hear again, *"Trust."*

So, I headed to the train station to purchase two bullet train tickets to Ishikawa Prefecture, where I would meet the long-awaited sound bowls, Zanmaikin, and the sound bowl creator, Mr. Kawakami. In spite of my worry, the man at the ticket counter easily finds the cheapest way to get there within my budget. I have plenty of time and money to tour historical places and enjoy the hotel where my dear friend, intuitive Travel Designer Cherie Rose Martin, booked for me and my daughter (who is a history major in college).

I haven't been on a bullet train heading towards the northwest side of Japan for decades, and it's the first time my daughter will visit another part of Japan besides Tokyo. We are heading to a place we have never been before called Komatsu.. We are excited to learn the history and I'm ecstatic to hear the real beauty of the Zanmaikin in person, not virtually. While we rapidly pass by the rice fields and the forest, I ask my Spirit Guides if I am supposed to be headed to Komatsu. I hear a clear voice saying, *"Trust. Return to your heritage."* I ask immediately, *"Komatsu is not my hometown nor my family...is it not the place to go for me?"*

I suddenly tasted some mint in my mouth and smelled roses. When I am confident and/or on the right path, I always taste mint and smell roses; it's been this way ever since I was a little girl. Even though I don't know anything about Komatsu, nor this sound bowl, I know I am supposed to be there and to trust the unknown. As soon as the thought of *"trust the unknown"* came through my mind, I heard the voice again: *"You will know in the morning."*

I giggle while my daughter gives me a weird look. My youngest likes to pull oracle cards from time to time, and one of her favorite cards says, *"You will know in the morning."*

As soon as we stepped out of the bullet train, we felt the warm and humid air flow through our bodies. I slip into the moment of deja vu again; a feeling of *"I have been here before"* flooded me, even though I knew I had never been to Komatsu before.

I call Mr. Kawakami, the creator of the sound bowl, to let him know that we are here. The closer I walk to his studio, the more my body starts to get comfortable; it's as if I'm coming home. As soon as I saw Mr. Kawakami and his wife's calm face, I felt like I had met them before. I may have come across them in one of my past lives.

I finally get to meet, touch, feel, and hear the vibration of the titanium sound bowls after a short but interesting story of how he created the Zanmaikin. The vibration that the Zanmaikin creates is literally out of this world.

Every sound wave is in the present, but it somehow feels like it's taking me to different places. I could spend all day there, showering myself in the sound and vibration of Zanmaikin. Even after the last sound I create, my body is still feeling the resonance.

I thought about whether or not to purchase the bowl. Even before I ask my Spirit Guides if it's a good purchase or not, again the flavor of mint spreads through my mouth and the scent roses flows through from nowhere.

I closed my eyes and clearly saw the number two. I trusted the number. I purchased two bowls. I knew that I'd be coming back. I have always loved music and playing musical instruments, but these sound bowls are just different. They make my body feel different. They are soothing and help me stay calm while simultaneously giving me energy. They are out of this world. I felt that I could have stayed there more than a few hours, but I knew it was time for me to go. So, I left; I carried all that had happened to me tucked in my heart.

During a nap in the bullet train back to my parent's house, I hear Spirit Guides whispering to me, *"Be ready. Trust. Returning to your heritage. Allow yourself to heal."* As I walk into my parents' home, my father tells me, *"Get ready to leave. We're going to my hometown as soon as your two daughters and your husband arrive."*

A few days later, we are back on a bullet train again. But this time, I'm with all three of my daughters and my husband (the only one missing is my son) and we're going to my father's hometown. It had been forty years for me; it was the first time with my family members.

My father had arranged to meet us at a hotel in Yonago, Tottori. I knew my father had been wanting to bring his grandchildren there for a long time, but I felt different sensations running through my body. My father told us to all dress properly and then led us to his car.

It seemed like he had made arrangements for us to spend time in our family graveyards. This was to recognize the existence of our ancestors, show some respect, and know where and who we came from. That's where I thought he was taking us: his family's graveyards. It seemed boring.

Instead, he took us to a temple called Shoumyouji where my grandfather, my father's father, belonged. He arranged for us to be there to attend the 50th anniversary of his passing. I was turning 50 years old, and 50 years had passed since he passed; he passed away before I even had a chance to meet him. He was waiting for me to come and visit him for the first time, but passed away a few days before my parents planned to bring me to see him for the first time.

I grew up hearing and thinking that my grandfather passed because he was working hard building something around the house for me so that I would be safe in the house. I had always felt bad and almost ashamed to want to know more about my grandfather, who I had never met. I was relieved that my father never talked deeply about his father's side of the family, but I always wondered what kind of person he was and how he might have been to me if he were alive (especially after my grandfather on my mother's side passed away).

As I walked into the temple where my grandfather had come many times before his passing, and as the head priest of the temple welcomed us, I noticed that I remembered the outside of the temple very well. It felt weird to feel comfortable and familiar as I walked into the temple with my husband and daughters.

Again, as the ceremony started with the sound bowl and chanting, I felt the unfamiliar feeling, energy, and beings around me. Before I decided to understand what it was, my family needed the translation of what the priest was saying to English for them to experience the ceremony completely.

"Trust. Allow yourself to feel. Release." I heard my Spirit Guides clearly whispering.

The priest said, *"Thank you very much for coming all the way from the United States. You step into the soil that all of your ancestors stepped in. You breathe the air that all of your ancestors breathed. Know that whatever you decide to do for the world, your ancestors are always with you and right by your side cheering you on. They are always ready to guide you whenever you need them. Your ancestors are not all deceased, but also living ones as well. They sit right next to you today. Ask, listen, so that you can step up to live your purposeful life, the life that you are meant to live. As you step out of this temple, please do not forget the moment that we shared today. And please, come back at any time. We are always here for you whether you are far or near."*

As I translate what the priest says, I feel the existence of all of my ancestors, including my father next to me and my grandfather who I have never met. I feel the massive group hug as the tears roll down my face. Again, the scent of roses filled the air, and the taste of mint spread in my mouth.

My father already had a place to take us and we followed his plan. He did not tell us where we are going. He took us to one of the oldest tombstone areas in Japanese history, Mukibanda. We went up the hill to see the tomb mounds and how the ancient Japanese may have lived. We walked up to the edge of the hill and sat on the bench overlooking the ocean. I take in how the peninsula is curved and how the ocean is quiet. I felt right away like I was in my recurring dream; the only difference is the sun is out instead of the moon.

My father never heard about my recurring dreams, and neither had my daughters, but I had been guided by my Spirit Guides to meet my ancestors and to start the process of healing. I stood right in front of the ocean where I had seen myself in my dreams all along. The ocean was dark in the dream, but light in the present.

My Spirit Guides knew all along that I would listen to the call to take this Spiritual Trip so I could learn to ask, listen, and take the inspiring action. So that I could take the responsibility to heal my past lives, my past with my ancestors, and step into my Divine Power.

There is no rose around me, but I again feel the smell of roses tickling my cheek while I taste the refreshing mint.

I continue to follow the smell of roses and the taste of mint. A year after spending profound time together with my ancestors, I now coach my clients on how to reconnect with their mind, body, and spirit. I teach them how to release and heal their mind, body, and spirit, and how to reclaim and return to their Divine Power. While I continue to be in this healing journey for myself, I also guide people to spend time with their Spirit Guides and Ancestors to reclaim their Divine Power and to live their unique, purposeful life. I am humbled and excited to experience healing with them every day, and I continue to send waves of love and hope to as many souls I can.

If you don't know why you are here on Earth or if you aren't clear what and who you are, start spending time with your Spirit Guides. Ask, listen, and take that inspired action. I assure you, your Spirit Guides and your Ancestors will be right by your side, cheering you on as you return to your True Self.

Reconnect, Release and Reclaim.

I am a healer that guides people to reconnect, to release and cleanse, to return and reclaim their Divine Power and their True Selves.

Returning to your heritage may help you find your way back to your truth. Your true self is connected to your Spirit Guides and your Ancestors, who are your biggest cheerleaders.

Are you ready?

ABOUT MAYUKO FUKINO

Mayuko was born in Tokyo, Japan and was raised in Japan and in the United States. Due to moving more than a few times between the countries, she grew up thinking she never belonged anywhere.

She was bullied when she was in elementary school in Japan and she always felt she wasn't accepted as she was; she felt different. She didn't feel like she belonged in the United States either because she felt behind academically, didn't feel like speaking English properly, and she felt different from others.

She continued to feel more lost in her life due to an accident on the busiest freeway in California, suffering from asthma and head-to-toe eczema in Japan, having four children while also having toxic relationships, losing a relationship with her son, leaving the toxic relationships, and moving across the country with teenagers. She realized that she has never left the connection with nature and with dance, music, and art.

As she committed to spend consistent and daily quiet time for herself throughout her training to become a yoga teacher, she became more aware of her body, her mind, and her spirit. When she asks questions, she receives clear answers visually in her dreams or meditation, either auditorily or sensorily.

After the spiritual trip she took, she realized her Spirit Guides and her Ancestors were right by her side all this time, and would even send people, books, or messages to give her what she needs to live her life fully in Divine Power. She is grateful for every person who came and will come across in her life.

Mayuko became a certified yoga and meditation teacher. As a Mind Body Spirit Wellness Coach, she teaches mindfulness and yoga at her local schools. She also coaches young adults and families to connect mind, body, and spirit through utilizing the five senses, yoga, movement, meditation, and energy healing modalities such as Ho'oponopono and Reiki. She works with lost souls, animals, and properties as well.

When she receives messages, she often channels them in dance, music, art and writing.

Mayuko lives in South Carolina where she can enjoy all four seasons and shares her life with her witty, adventurous, and amazing cook and husband, Bruce, two beautiful and caring teenage daughters, and two energetic Australian Shepherd dogs that sometimes think they are deer. She also loves FaceTime visits with her musician son who lives in Los Angeles, and visits from her oldest daughter who enjoys the political scene in New York. She enjoys learning, reading, hiking, traveling, eating different foods, and meeting new people.

Her mission is to live fully and truly of her Divine Power and Truth, to love, to share, and to guide others to discover and live their Divine Power and Truth for a loving and peaceful world.

She is very excited to step into a new role as a travel designer to bring healing and more love for people and for places as they travel near or far.

To connect with Mayuko:

Facebook: @MayukoTLC365

Instagram: @mindfulmayuko

Website: www.mindfullifestyledesign.com

Email: mindfulmayuko@gmail.com

The Road to Mr. Right

Jamie DeMarco

I ALWAYS WANTED MY OWN PRINCE CHARMING. I ALWAYS wanted the fairytale.

Most people will tell you that fairytales don't exist - that happily ever afters are unrealistic.

But I can tell you from experience…They're wrong.

INTRO

I've never cried so hard in my life. Sitting in a random Trader Joe's parking lot, polishing off my second box of tissues, I attempted to accept that my five-year relationship was officially over. To be honest, I'd known the relationship was far past its expiration date, but that didn't stop the tearful, ugly, blubbering meltdown.

As I cried, I eventually realized that I wasn't even that sad about the relationship ending. I'd known things hadn't been great for a while. I actually *chose* to end my turbulent relationship. I actually *chose* to be single. At least, I thought I knew what I was doing. As I rummaged around for my emergency purse tissues though, it became blatantly clear that I was quite a floundering, broken, hot mess.

Truthfully, I was baffled by my intense emotional reaction. I didn't understand where it was coming from. In my mind, the breakup loomed for a year before it's unavoidable finale. I discussed and debated my options at length. I took everything and everyone into consideration. I looked at possibilities and options from every angle. I understood the full weight of my choice, and I knew that broken leases, abandoned plans, and shattered future dreams were just the start of what undoubtedly would be a rough few months.

Ultimately though, I felt sure in the decision to part ways. I was ready to move on with my life. I was hopeful, optimistic and genuinely looking forward to beginning again. Hell, I was even excited to get back out on the dating scene (eventually).

However, to my dismay, the water works persisted. I checked the rearview mirror and almost laughed at what stared back at me. Red, puffy, slit-like eyes. Rats nest hair. A shirt so wet it looked as though I dumped a bottle of water on myself. Holy crap - was I actually *in public* right now?! That's embarrassing, but more importantly I couldn't help thinking, *"What in the world is wrong with me? Didn't I ASK for this?"*

Where was this intense, overwhelming feeling coming from?

Then it hit me like a ton of bricks.

It was TERROR.

Untethered, free-flowing terror just POURING out of me in the grocery store parking lot...*great.*

I knew that this terror was just a (hopefully fleeting) feeling, but the terror was REAL. And I'd never experienced anything like it. I was freaking terrified! TER-RI-FIED. I just knew it. I was scared shitless. *But why?!?*

Shaking and attempting to process, it finally all clicked.

I was terrified...of being **alone.**

Once acknowledged, it was like a knife to the gut.

I was going to be alone. Alone for a long time. Alone after five years of constant comfort and companionship.

Alone in a new city. Without many close friends. Full of regret.

That decision to quit my job six months ago so I could "find my calling"? Yeah...*that* sure didn't seem quite as brilliant anymore.

Welp. There it was. Alone in what felt like ALL aspects of life, I was **afraid** of being on my own, and I found myself in complete paralyzing fear over how I'd ever fix my busted-up life.

EPIPHANY

Straightening, I looked back in the mirror. Forcing myself to ignore my haggardness (and a few staring shoppers), I geared up for a much needed, self-motivational pep talk.

I was a successful, competitive, independent woman! I had surmounted many obstacles in my day, overcame adversity, and took tons of brave first steps (solo!). This chapter of my life is no different!

Yes, I was sure in my decision to end things. Yes, I was sure I was meant for something better. I KNEW there was a perfect guy out there for me that would also give me the relationship I desired. As a proud Pisces, I was *certain* I'd fall into a spectacularly romantic, fairytale-esque, happily ever after love story one day.

Letting my Prince Charming fantasy play out in my head, the tears finally stopped.

I could see the future and it was bright! I would totally have that incredible relationship next. I would meet Mr. Right, we'd fall in love, and have a blissful fairytale romance! We'd have an extraordinary, lasting relationship, and we'd be completely, joyously fulfilled in every area of life. I couldn't wait! Rings, weddings and babies? Yes, please!

Was I getting ahead of myself? *Absolutely!* But, I didn't care.

Always a big dreamer, I loved drawing out all the details in my fantasy world. I was jumping for joy over meeting this "Perfect Man" that would undoubtedly be "The One."

As I began literally listing out all of the qualities I wanted in a man, I started to become aware that this perfect guy was well, perfect! Intelligent, funny and generous? Check, check and check! Ambitious and goal oriented? Sounds great! He'd obviously also be tall, dark, and ridiculously handsome...and have a bad boy look, but actually be a caring romantic. Oh, and he'd be assertive, a leader, and stand up for himself while simultaneously treating me like a princess. Lovely! That's not too hard to come by, right?!

In the midst of enjoying my Dream Guy daydream, I had a stark, unpleasant realization.

This "ideal man" *really* had his life together.

And I...well, did NOT.

My future "dream guy" was financially stable, accomplished, passionate about his career, super-hot and fit, family-oriented, had a supportive community, an incredible house, was fulfilled in life, relationship-ready and just waiting for Ms. Right to show up.

I was jobless, broke, and utterly single. I had *no clue* about who I was, what I wanted, or **anything** regarding my next steps in life.

Comparing my current world to Mr. Dreamy's, it was painfully obvious that his life situation was great, and that mine was crap. So **why** was I expecting this wonderful Prince Charming to magically show up, rescue me from my tearful abyss and solve all of my problems? Honestly, how could I expect my Dream Man to even *like* me at this point? Let alone fall in love, propose with a 2+ karat diamond and live out my fairytale happily ever after anytime soon. Even the most delusional part of me knew that was *never going to happen. Ouch...*

Things seemed super, *super* bleak, but I had an epiphany.

If I wanted a Dream Guy with all the qualities I was looking for - that had his life together - *and* was ready and looking for a relationship - then I NEEDED TO HAVE MY LIFE TOGETHER, TOO!

Ah ha!!! Finally, a starting point. A light at the end of this crazily dark, teary-eyed tunnel!

My frayed mind started to piece together that Dream Guys (at least the ones I wanted) were **high-quality men.** They were the: top of the barrel, super fulfilled in life, borderline-Alpha Gods that were ready to sweep a lucky girl off her feet and provide her with an epic romance and lasting love story one day. (And yes, Thor, Captain America and Superman are all perfectly acceptable Dream Man examples.)

On further thought, I realized that these high-quality men had *already* done the extensive legwork to make their *own* lives amazing...so why would they want someone who's still figuring out step one? More likely than not, a desperate, unsure, clueless-in-life woman would be a turn *off* to a man who's already so fulfilled.

Pondering it all...it hit me.

Sure, a Dream Guy probably wouldn't pursue a jobless, insecure damsel, but he WOULD most likely be into another fulfilled, satisfied and happy-in-life Dream **GIRL!**

Of course!!! Feeling the fog lift and the wheels churning, I finally figured it out...

I just needed to be...drum roll please...a **DREAM GIRL!**

Aka, a high-quality woman!

Aka, a woman with her life together!

GENIUS.

Only one problem...

I had NO CLUE how to just, "get my life together!" I didn't even know how to take the first step!

Instead of curling up with a tub of ice-cream, I made a choice.

I DECIDED TO BE BRAVE.

Yes, I was scared, lonely, and on my own for the first time in what felt like FOREVER, but I mark that moment as the day my whole life changed course.

Armed with a semi-crushed (or semi-hopeful?) plan for the future, I swiped the final tears away, fervently clicked in my seatbelt, and drove into the unknown, absolutely terrifying (but also invigorating) world of: *Single Status.*

Although I was somewhat prepared for what was bound to be a lengthy stretch in companionless-land, I won't lie. Single life is ROUGH. There were dark days. There were more tears (obviously). I learned a lot by clumsy trial and error.

However, (eventually…) I reinvented myself. I boldly (albeit scaredly) decided to try new things. I enrolled in Career Coaching. I read what felt like a billion self-development books. I volunteered. I went back to my roots and pursued childhood passions. And as I learned more about this new version of myself, I started becoming confident in who I authentically was at my core.

Half the time I didn't know what I was doing, and I definitely did not have my entire life path figured out (still don't!), but I at least knew the general direction to go. *Side note - that direction is simply: forward.*

"Just figure your life out" eventually turned into "Do what makes you happy," then, "Follow Your Dreams," and finally, "Accomplish Your Goals".

Of course, there were setbacks and unexpected obstacles, but I just **kept going.** I pushed through the rough patches. I forgave myself after slip ups, meltdowns and far too much ice cream and wine. I was kind and loving to myself. I slowly made progress in all areas of my life, and started becoming a woman that any friend, man or family member would be proud to know.

It took me three years, tons of research, coaching, counseling, and *lots* of dating, but I finally figured it out. I'd learned who I truly was. I had clarity on my life and relationship goals. I knew exactly what I wanted and needed in a relationship (and also what I *didn't* want or need). I had high standards, and was actually totally fine being single for once.

I was also seriously at the top of my game. Those three years of pure self-development looked GOOD on me. I'm talking - best shape of my adult life, ridiculously confident, master's degree in hand, starting my dream job & living in an amazing new walkable city - level of awesomeness. My life was amazing! I was happy and I LOVED myself. I felt truly irresistible.

Needless to say, I was a changed woman. And I can honestly tell you – when I decided to invest time, energy and effort into MYSELF; when I decided to actually put ME first for once – *that* was the moment everything shifted.

I stopped attracting the "players/cheaters/guys not ready for a commitment", and started attracting relationship-ready MEN. I completely changed the way I dated and therefore, how guys treated me. I became a pro at navigating the online dating scene and opened my inbox to dozens of emails daily. Although I had lots of suitors and plenty of opportunities to fall into a decent relationship, I held out.

I wanted the Prince Charming Dream Guy! I wanted the Fairytale. I knew I was a catch and would never settle again. I had a lot to offer "The One".

I was FINALLY that *Dream Girl* I'd envisioned in the Trader Joe's parking lot all those years ago. A Dream Girl that any high-quality, Dream Guy would be lucky to have.

I just knew my fairytale was coming soon - I FELT it, deep in my soul. I was where I was meant to be and honestly felt on top of the world.

I was confident with a capital C and was ready for Mr. Right to make his appearance, ASAP.

But to my dismay, I was still...painfully, single-ly, alone. I mean I had a great life, job and friend group but HELLO! MR. PRINCE CHARMING! I'm BEYOND ready for you! Feel free to keep taking FOREVER!!!

At this point, I'd been working on myself and patiently waiting for Mr. Right for THREE YEARS now. Where the heck was he?!

MANIFEST

Back to the drawing board, I decided to do some reflecting on these years of growth and development to see if I could piece together any conclusions.

I didn't realize it at the time, but all these years I'd been manifesting my dream life! Sure, there was hard work and some luck involved, but I recognized that the process of: figure out what makes you happy, pursue your passions, accomplish your goals - is a pretty brilliant life plan!

There was only one complication. No matter how much I proudly flaunted my Type A, "I can achieve anything with a plan!" way of being, I *still* couldn't control the fact that there was no step-by-step guide on how to "accomplish the goal" of finding Mr. Right and living out my happily ever after.

I mean, I knew I was meant to have my dream relationship and that it would happen one day soon, but I couldn't just sign up to earn a "I'm a Dream Girl and Now Deserve a Dream Man" Degree and expect Prince Charming on my doorstep the next day. There was no way to buy, earn, borrow or steal a Dream Man. So how did one *actually* get the relationship they desire?

Frustrated I couldn't conjure up my Mr. Right with the click of a button, I threw up my hands, took a deep, positivity-infused breath, and reminded myself whatever's meant to be - WILL BE.

SERENDIPITY

Oh, The Universe...how it works in mysterious, absolutely fascinating ways. The timing and perfectly ordered events leading up to two destined lovers' crossed paths is quite the enigma - and its astonishing how things "just happen" to magically work out (typically beyond our wildest expectations!) once your life is aligned.

I would know...because sure enough, once everything in my life clicked into place, IT HAPPENED.

No lie, on the precise afternoon I *finally* felt: secure within my authentic self, accomplished in life, confident in my ability to crush my new, amazing dream job, and like there wasn't a single other goal I could possibly achieve...I MET HIM.

Well, I accidentally stole his seat at a random bar. A bar in my town that I never went to (and didn't like), but felt oddly inspired to check out that Friday afternoon. At a bar that was so packed, I almost turned around and left. Twice...

At a bar that, as it turns out, HE didn't really like and never went to, either.

And wouldn't you believe...we met at that random, semi-gross bar on what happened to be the EXACT AFTERNOON that HE (for the first time in **years**), was fully single, happy, complete, and ready to find the one, TOO.

Sparks flew, banter was thrown, drinks were had. I cautiously agreed to a date (hey I just met this guy - he could be a creeper), and we planned to meet up a few days later.

Date Day arrived. I didn't have my hopes up (as I'd blown through hundreds of first dates with guys that turned out to be subpar), and I went into the evening without any expectations besides enjoying a free meal with a hot, ripped, hilarious guy.

We sat down, started talking and....didn't stop. Literally, we just kept passionately talking about our lives, experiences and goals. We grew off each other's excitement, and were SO into (the *four hours*) of chatting with each other that we completely forgot to eat. The restaurant closed and we realized we'd never even ordered food!

Our excitement, passion and enthusiasm grew so much by just *talking* to each other...that in that moment, we both just knew.

We KNEW - that we'd *both* just found The One.

INSPIRE

People may say true love is fated, or destined, but that doesn't mean we should just chill in the backseat of life's ride expecting romance miracles. While I *do* believe in some higher power that may help us along our paths, I firmly believe that **we** create our own journey. WE are in the driver's seat. Our CHOICES determine our actions and therefore what type of life we lead.

A lot of people say that they found the love of their life when they weren't expecting it, or hear of couples connecting only when the timing was *exactly* right for both parties to meet. While I absolutely believe that all things happen for a reason, and there's a ton we *can't* control, I also believe that we *choose* to design our own lives.

WE get to design our destiny.

The day Matt and I split a bar stool was also the first day I felt completely satisfied in my own life as an individual. I worked *hard* to get to that point. I'd accomplished goals. I finally landed my Dream Job. I dealt with the emotions, stress, nerves and roadblocks that inevitably appear when making all those scary changes. I battled through, aimed for the stars and landed in a place that, albeit wasn't what I expected, I was proud as hell to be standing at. Loud sports bar or not, **I had arrived.** My life was in place. I was (singly) complete.

It was literally the PERFECT day for me to meet the man I'd spend the rest of my life with. And coincidently (or not?) it was the perfect day for Matt to meet the woman *he'd* spend the rest of his life with, too. Serendipity? Fate?

Or...a little luck combined with blazoned determination? We may never truly know...

CONCLUSION

So, how'd this epic love story end?

Well, pretty spectacularly, if I do say so myself.

On our first date, we were so engrossed in conversation with each other we literally forgot to eat dinner.

By our third date, we both knew that we were each other's "one," though we both thought it on our first.

By week two, I'd concluded that Matt checked EVERY. SINGLE. BOX on my Trader Joe's Dream Man list.

Within our first month of dating, I love yous were exchanged.

By month three, I was at his place more often than mine.

We moved in together after six months, and began looking at engagement rings in month number nine...his idea, I swear!

A year after we met, he proposed. (And yes, the ring he selected also surpassed my wildest dreams, too!)

On 5.15.15 (cute, right?), we were MARRIED on a beautiful, luxurious rooftop overlooking the turquoise ocean in Riviera Maya, Mexico. *Swoon.*

I married my Dream Man in the most picturesque setting imaginable, with more than I possibly could have imagined, surrounded by 46 of my family members and closest friends. I had my dream pink, white and black-tie fairytale wedding, complete with a ball gown princess dress (hell if I care that we were sweating in Mexico!), and the most amazing wedding week EVER (yes, I also made my wedding into a week-long event). Matt and I had an incredibly romantic honeymoon traveling on a luxury cruise liner throughout Europe and ate and laughed our way through eleven different countries together.

Half a decade later, and Matt still treats me like a princess, gives me a platform to completely be myself, and showers me with so much love and adoration daily, it makes me blush writing this.

Matt makes me feel so special and loved. He's my rock, my partner, my other half. We completely complement each other; we make the other better, and grow in all aspects of our lives every day.

We live in our dream house - an all window, 21st floor modern oasis overlooking DC, with views for days and where life in the clouds is our daily reality. We're both working our dream jobs (remotely!), and spend tons of time together laughing, cooking, and binge-watching Netflix. The loving relationship we have is way better than anything I could've imagined, and to top it off – I absolutely LOVE my life.

I'm not going to lie; I've known for a while that any guy would be lucky to have me (no confidence problems here!) – but I'm the luckiest girl in the world to have HIM.

THE FAIRYTALE LIFE

Basking in the complete bliss that is my current life status, I'm grateful to that broken girl that once was. If it wasn't for one of the lowest times in my life, I'd have never gained the courage to embrace the fear, pick up the pieces and start anew. If it wasn't for my Trader Joe's meltdown, I'm not sure the tearful "Just become a Dream Girl worthy of a Dream Guy" moment would have even happened. Without that epiphany, I don't think I would have had the strength to keep pushing and bettering myself throughout the years, and who knows where I'd be today.

Even though it's over a decade later, that semi-shameful parking lot moment is still cemented in my mind like it was yesterday. Not because of the heartache (uh, sorry ex!), but because in that dark moment, unbeknownst to me at the time, I was struck with the inspiration that would ultimately lead me to my dream life, my happily ever after, and my mission in this world.

There's something miraculous about finding the intersection between your passion and your calling. Difficult to discover, yes, but once found, life changing.

My story is inspirational. Aspirational. Hell, still even to myself to this day. However, there's a greater purpose in life that exists beyond just figuring out our *own* life path or purpose. In addition to the astounding potential we have as individuals, we also have unique, specific talents that we're meant to *share* with this world. So, these days, while living blissfully with my beyond-incredible husband, in our gorgeous house in the clouds, amidst our self-made, perfect dream life, I still get inspired every single day - by helping thousands of women find *their* own fairytales and happily ever afters, too.

Quite the dream life, indeed.

I always wanted my own Prince Charming. I always wanted the fairytale.

Most people will tell you that fairytales don't exist - that happily ever afters are unrealistic.

But I can tell you from experience…They're wrong.

You CAN Have Your Dream Man, Your Dream Relationship, Your Dream Life.

You can have your Prince Charming.

You can have your fairytale ending (and wedding!).

You CAN have it all.

IT JUST STARTS WITH YOU.

ABOUT JAMIE DEMARCO

Jamie, aka "Your Real Life Fairy Godmother," is a Dating & Relationship Coach, Matchmaker, and founder of Find Your Fairytale. A travel enthusiast, yogi and aspiring photographer, Jamie's free time is typically spent cozied up, planning her next breathtaking adventure with a glass of wine, vegan ice cream, and her princess-diva cat, Lily.

Growing up as a top-ranked competitive gymnast, Jamie demonstrated the drive and determination to be successful even as a child. After a career ending knee injury, Jamie continued to help others become successful in the sport by spending seven years as a sought-after gymnastics coach. Her desire to be the best combined with her natural leadership skills served her well once she graduated college, as she landed a Regional Sales Director position at twenty-one years old.

Jamie has since become a top performer, manager, and leader in the sales, fitness, and education industries, and has excelled in positions such as Area Sales Director, Sales Advisor, and Sr. Admissions Counselor. Although Jamie quickly proved herself as a top performer and leader in her previous roles, each time she reached the top of a company, she felt a familiar tug in her heart. Though she didn't know what, she knew she was meant for something more. Jamie wanted passion in her life and career, and she wanted to uniquely make an impact in the world.

After she left her last 9-5 job to pursue her dreams, Jamie completed a Master's Degree in Academic Advising, became a Certified Professional Coach (CPC) through The Institute for Professional Excellence in Coaching (iPEC), earned an Associate Certified Coach (ACC) credential through the International Coach Federation (ICF), and obtained an Energy Leadership Master Practitioner Certification (ELI-MP). She met her Prince Charming by accidentally stealing his seat in 2012, had her dream wedding in 2015, and is now living a fairytale life of great love and epic travel adventures with her amazing husband, Matt.

Once she created her dream life, (and figured out "the secret" to dating, love, and how to attract high-quality partners!), Jamie combined her Sales, Advising, and Life Coaching expertise to create Find Your Fairytale - an international company that helps women confidently snag their dream men, have extraordinary relationships, and become absolutely irresistible.

Jamie's mission is to help women become the bold, radiant queens they were always meant to be so they can start living the life and love story of their dreams. She's all about empowering women to stand up for what they want and need in relationships, live on their own terms, and to be treated the way they deserve in their love life. Jamie's greatest desire is to help others find their fairytale and have their happily ever after.

Just like she did...

When she's not helping women snag their dream guy, Jamie enjoys indulging in The Bachelor, binge reading self-development and dystopian future audio books, and fully embracing her Piscean-nature by floating in the ocean and/or her bathtub.

Jamie can't wait to meet you, inspire you to be your most amazing self, and help you have the epic love story you've always deserved.

To connect with Jamie (& Get Free Confidence Secrets!) go to:

www.findyourfairytale.com

Jamie@findyourfairytale.com

Instagram: www.instagram.com/jamieedemarco

Facebook: www.facebook.com/jamieedemarco

LinkedIn: www.linkedin.com/in/jamieedemarco

Would you like to publish your
story in a collaboration piece?

We are now putting together...
She is Magic, YES!
... (Book Four of the Series)

Spots are now open for you to join
us and share your story of magic
with the world.

Please connect with us
through the link below for
more information:

https://blairhayse.kartra.com/
page/blairhaysepublishing

Made in the USA
Columbia, SC
21 February 2021

33360136R00215